ACKNOWLEDGMENTS

THE author would like to thank the following, for their kindness in giving permission for the use of copyright material : George Allen & Unwin Ltd., for extracts from *The Analysis of Mind*, by Bertrand Russell; Professor A. J. Ayer, for extracts from *The Foundations of Empirical Knowledge*; The Bobbs-Merrill Co. Inc., for extracts from *The Structure of Appearance*, by Nelson Goodman, © 1966 by The Bobbs-Merrill Co. Inc.; and Professor G. Ryle, for extracts from *Mind*.

ERRATA

Page vii, last line to read *Index of Philosophers' Names*   214
Page 42, line 4 : *for* end-on *read* head-on
Page 184, line 16 : delete comma after ' is '
Page 186, line 8 : delete comma after ' are '

A CRITIQUE OF BRITISH EMPIRICISM

FRASER COWLEY

MACMILLAN
LONDON · MELBOURNE · TORONTO
ST MARTIN'S PRESS
NEW YORK
1968

© Fraser Cowley 1968

Published by
MACMILLAN AND CO LTD
Little Essex Street London W C 2
and also at Bombay Calcutta and Madras
Macmillan South Africa (Publishers) Pty Ltd Johannesburg
The Macmillan Company of Australia Pty Ltd Melbourne
The Macmillan Company of Canada Ltd Toronto
St Martin's Press Inc New York

Library of Congress catalog card no. 68–10754

Printed in Great Britain by
R. & R. CLARK, LTD., EDINBURGH

TO MY FATHER

CONTENTS

vii

INTRODUCTION

THE standpoint from which my criticisms of empiricist philosophy are made is phenomenological, in the sense given to that word by Husserl. But they owe much more to Sartre and Merleau-Ponty. Reflexive or phenomenological analysis in my terms concerns our experience, as embodied beings in the world, of things and others in the world.

The " thesis of the world " or natural attitude – in Hume's terms, the natural belief in the independent existence of the world – is unthinking, unreasoned, and inseparable from our being embodied subjects in the world. It is not in any ordinary sense a belief. What we believe to be the case or not to be the case, what we believe to exist or not to exist, presupposes the world and our own bodily being in it. Empiricism characteristically postulates some other starting-point for the analysis of experience and thence attempts to construct or reconstruct the self, the world and the things in the world. The perennial problem is the nature of the starting-point, the indubitable or incorrigible data. There are no such data. But the interesting question, which I attempt to disentangle, is why it was thought there were, or must be, such data.

The model of explanation which is applied by empiricist philosophy to our ordinary unreflecting experience of being in the world, situated in the midst of things, is borrowed from ordinary factual and scientific knowledge which takes this experience for granted. We explain things, events and processes by formulating hypotheses and testing them by observation. In doing this we take the world and our being in the world for granted, and we take the things we actually see and observe for our data, our starting-point. Empiricism tries to apply the same method to show how we arrive at this starting-point, or to show how the world and things we observe can be analysed into, or constructed out of, the real or immediate data, which are not things, events or processes of the ordinary observable kind in the world. These latter are regarded by Hume not as data but as objects of belief or " fictions of the imagination ", and as posits, postulates or logical constructions by his successors.

This procedure, I believe, cannot be understood apart from the physical and physiological theories in which the concept of a sensation or perception, a mental event or an event in consciousness, originated. These theories which of course took things in the world for granted – bodies in particular – are in fact premises of Hume's doctrine of impressions and ideas. Yet the impressions and ideas are taken to be the actual data out of which the physical world is constructed by the imagination and belief.

My procedure is to examine empiricist doctrines in four representative works : Hume's *Treatise*, Russell's *The Analysis of Mind*, Ayer's *The Foundations of Empirical Knowledge* and Ryle's *The Concept of Mind*. I also examine Nelson Goodman's discussion of physicalism and phenomenalism in *The Structure of Appearance*.[1] The only feasible way was to take each philosopher in turn, since their doctrines, though closely related, are far from identical. The effect of doing so is that topics and arguments are not kept neatly apart, but recur in different contexts. I hope this is a virtue as well as a necessity. I want to show that perceiving, feeling, doing and saying cannot be understood in isolation from each other, and that our experience of things in the world cannot be understood apart from our experience of being bodily in the midst of them. The point of reflexive analysis is to make explicit what is implicit in our experience; the point of making distinctions is to show how experience hangs together, and, incidentally, to show the impossibility of a reductive analysis.

For Hume the only possible analysis is a reductive analysis. The relations of impressions and ideas are external: " Anything may be joined to anything." Hence his fundamental dogma that what is distinguishable is separable and what is not separable is not distinguishable. This assumption operates far beyond the classic context in which he discusses it – the colour and shape of a visible thing. The concept of

---

[1] I hope no one will mind my including an American empiricist in a work of this title.

a " perception " is the prime example. In the perception, the perceiving and the perceived, experience and what is experienced, the
consciousness of an object and the object of consciousness, are identified.
For since they are inseparable, they must be identical. The perception
is then, however, regarded as itself an object – for Hume must talk of
the perceptions which he *has* – but so to speak, as a subjective or
" private " object, an intramental object, an " internal and perishing
existence ".

Two hundred years later, the main point in philosophising about
perception is still for Ayer, as it was for Hume, " to analyse the relation
of our sense-experiences to the propositions we put forward concerning
material things ". These sense-experiences or contents or perceptions
or sense-data, as Ayer variously calls them, are the direct descendants
of Hume's impressions and ideas. The distinction between our experience of something and the something we experience and their
inseparable connection is further illustrated in my examination of
Goodman's discussion of physicalism and phenomenalism.

Of central importance to the classic empiricist position is the treatment of appearances or looks of things as objects or indeed as quasi-
things. I have called this the " illusion of real appearances ". My
account of this mistake and my discussion of depth perception and the
constancies of size and shape follow Merleau-Ponty's acute analysis in
his chapter ' L'Espace ' in *La Phénoménologie de la perception*. They
are closely related to my analysis on Sartrean lines of mental images
and " the illusion of immanence ".

Ryle stands somewhat apart from the other philosophers I discuss.
He often engages in phenomenological analysis, even if it be *malgré lui*,
and I am in full agreement with a great deal of what he has to say. But
the crucial distinction of subject and object is no less apt to be conjured
away in his hands. To put the point somewhat crudely: in his account
of self-knowledge and knowledge of others, it is as if all selves were
others and all others were objects. It is not, however, as such that we
have experience of others nor as such that we understand them. It is
because our spontaneous understanding and insight, the affectivity
and empathy from which these are inseparable, and our teleological
explanation of their conduct as of our own, do not constitute objective

knowledge as this has been understood since the rise of natural science that they are rejected by scientific psychologists – behaviourists and stimulus-response theorists in particular – who are concerned to find causal explanations. Ryle is largely concerned with how we make sense of what people are up to and know the sort of people they are. But explanation in terms of dispositions, in his account, is in effect causal explanation, and this is closely connected with the behaviourist tendency in his account of mind. I also argue that his view that men are not machines is based on an old-fashioned concept of mechanisms and machines, and that his objective criteria for saying that behaviour is intelligent or that the agent is thinking what he is doing can be applied directly to some machines.

In Ryle's account of "knowing how and knowing that", we understand what people are doing, what they are up to, in a sense closely analogous to that in which we understand what they say or what they mean. That is to say, we make sense of their actions and conduct as well as of their utterances. "Understanding is a part of knowing *how*" (*Concept* p. 54). "Roughly, execution and understanding are merely different exercises of knowledge of the tricks of the same trade." One might be inclined to say that speaking a language and understanding it were indeed a perfect example of this, but by no means a unique example: for not only do we make sense or fail to make sense of conduct, situations, happenings and events, but we are also quite often inclined to call them significant or insignificant, and in the case of conduct rational or senseless.

But for Ryle, and for many other philosophers, meaning is simply the meaning or sense that established expressions in the language have, and his professed business is the logical grammar and conceptual analysis of "mental" terms. Happily, he does not stick to his business as he professes it, and in my view he could not do so.

There is a complex of meanings of "meaning" whose interrelations it is of fundamental importance to elucidate. One of these is what is called intentionality in the literature of phenomenology. When we are thinking of something, looking at something, imagining something, what we have in mind or in view is what we mean or "intend". If, for example, I point someone out to a friend, he may ask : "You mean the man in the red scarf?" and I may reply: "No, I mean the one in the blue coat." The man I have in view is the man I mean or "intend", my looking at him is my meaning or intending that man, and in speech I refer to the man I mean.

Now the referring description which I use, "the man in the blue coat", has a sense or meaning; in using it to refer to the man before me I am expressing my meaning, or in other words, I am meaning it, meaning what I say: the meaning or sense of the expression "the man in the blue coat" is my present meaning. To understand the connection of my meaning the man and my meaning what I say is important for understanding the nature of language and thought and their relation to perceiving, imagining and doing.

When we look at anything, what we see is not just a "this" but a "such". We see it *as* such-and-such, we see a universal *in re*, or we see the object under a certain description. This last way of putting the point is perhaps the most suggestive: for whatever we see or otherwise experience, and however we experience it, can be said. For us talking animals the two are inseparable. In practice we do not even bother to distinguish what we observe from our statement or description.

I have tried to elucidate these questions in the later chapters. I have been led to the conclusion that sense-experience, except as a general term for seeing, hearing, etc., is a useless concept. In looking and seeing we are getting things sorted out and organised in our purview. Perceiving is making sense of things by the senses. Hearing what someone says or reading a book are special cases of this.

My debt to Merleau-Ponty cannot be adequately indicated in particular references. This is not, however, a study of his doctrines but a critique of empiricism in terms which, I hope, empiricists may easily understand. In addition to his treatment of depth perception and appearances which I have referred to above, I would also mention in particular his chapter 'Le corps comme expression et comme la parole' in the same work, *La Phénoménologie de la perception*. I hope I may have helped to naturalise in English some of this excellent philosopher's insights.

I have found Husserl's most interesting comments on Hume and

British empiricism in the volume *Erste Philosophie* (1923/4), I (*Husserliana*, vol. vii. Martinus Nijhoff). The fundamental study of psychologism is in the *Logische Untersuchungen*, and my treatment of what I have chosen to call naturalistic fallacies – in spite of Moore's pre-emption of the term – is more or less derived from this. Lastly, I would mention among the works which I have found illuminating Norman Kemp Smith's masterly study *The Philosophy of David Hume* (Macmillan, 1941) and C. V. Salmon's *The Central Problem of David Hume's Philosophy* (Max Niemeyer, 1929), an offprint from Husserl's *Jahrbuch*, vol. x.

I would like to express my thanks to Dr G. E. Davie of Edinburgh University for his invaluable comments on each chapter and his constant encouragement.

Queen's University F. C.
Kingston, Ontario

CHAPTER ONE

NATURE AND HUMAN NATURE

AFTER Newton, natural philosophy dominated metaphysics. The world of direct experience, the lived world, came to be regarded as a collection of minor effects of the great machine upon one small but complicated part of it, the body, and apprehended by a mind which was essentially disembodied. These effects were the so-called impressions or sensations. In Locke's doctrine, the distinction was made between the mind and its materials, the ideas, and between the ideas and their " original " or source, which he assumed to be external, physical objects. These objects affect the senses and " they from external objects convey into the mind what produces there those perceptions ", i.e. the ideas (*Essay*, Bk. II i 3).

This neat scheme fell apart on one main ground: if ideas were the materials and the only materials of the mind, and if all relations including causal relations were relations between ideas, no knowledge of the original or source of these ideas was possible. For the objects of physics, anatomy and physiology could be nothing but ideas. What Locke meant here and in other contexts, though not always, by " the senses " were those objects of anatomy, the external sense organs, the nervous system and the brain. And what could they themselves be but ideas?

But Locke's most far-reaching influence arose from his failure to stick to this doctrine, his failure to realise what it entailed, and his failure to realise that he had departed from it. " Sensation " often means not the process whereby an idea is produced, but the idea itself. And the idea and the sensation are frequently identified with the sensible quality of an object, as we perceive it, for example the brown of the table-top. This confusion is not due at bottom to Locke's obvious and notorious carelessness about his terms, but to his inveterate realism. The theory of representative perception suffers from the entirely unphilosophical, but fatal, flaw that no one has ever succeeded in holding it. The " holding " of the theory has generally been confined to the propounding of it. Once propounded, it is forgotten.

Locke forgets it constantly. When he speaks of a sensible object about which our senses are conversant, it is quite uncertain whether he means our complex idea or the cause of it. And it does not really matter which he means, except where he is formally propounding the distinction. Whichever he formally means, what he invariably has in mind is the sort of thing we can see and touch – a chair, a grain of wheat, a lump of gold. It is useless to ask Locke: is a chair a complex idea or its original? Officially, his answer is: the chair differs from the complex idea, which it produces by its affection of the senses, only in its lack of colour, warmth or coolness, smell and possible other simple ideas. These ideas are caused by the secondary qualities in the body, which have no resemblance to them but are defined as the power to produce them.

How could Locke have failed to see that the distinctions between the original and the idea and between primary and secondary qualities are untenable? Only by ignoring them. This seems a paradoxical thing to say, for it is obviously an essential part of his doctrine and the part which his successors fell upon. Locke ostensibly makes much of it, and when he forgets it occasionally calls himself to order and makes obeisance to it. But when, for example, Locke says: " Take a grain of wheat, divide it into two parts, each part has still solidity, extension, figure, and mobility; . . . and so divide it on, till the parts become insensible; they must retain still each of them all those qualities ", it is an actual, visible, tangible grain to which he is obviously referring. Is this grain, which he might hold in his hand and look at, the thing itself, or a complex idea? It could make not the slightest difference what his answer was. It makes not the slightest difference when he says " quality " where he ought to say " idea ", or " sensation " where he ought to say " idea " or " quality ". His incorrigible realism makes them interchangeable.

As Hume was to point out, " The philosophical system acquires all its influence on the imagination from the vulgar one ". Its advantage " is its similarity to the vulgar one; by which means we can humour our reason for a moment, when it becomes troublesome and solicitous; and yet upon its least negligence or inattention, can easily return to our vulgar and natural notions" (*Treatise*, pp. 213, 216). Locke's vulgar and natural notions are everywhere evident in the rest of the *Essay*. But so are Hume's in the *Treatise*, and his system, as we shall see, stands upon the same foundation.

The sensations in the mind, for Locke, are equivalent to knowledge of sensible qualities or to " perceptions of things " possessing these qualities.

For Locke, however, the mind was not identified with its ideas or sensations. In subsequent sensationalist doctrines it was, though imperfectly and without consistency. The term " sensation " suffered from a hopeless ambiguity, and still does. It was both a physiological occurrence and a conscious or experienced occurrence. Even when it did not mean both things at once, it passed easily and freely from the one meaning to the other.

This confusion is entirely natural, and is one of a number of related confusions which are still common at the present day. Central to the confusions are the bodily sensations – pain, cold, heat, hunger, shivering, itching, tension, etc. These are felt in, or on, the body in direct experience. They are conscious experiences, i.e. we feel them, and they are bodily experiences, i.e. they are located precisely or vaguely somewhere between top and toe. When we attend to them or when they force themselves on our attention, they are experienced as the figure, but most of the time they are the background to our activities. Such sensations, however, are essentially experienced, and we can always attend to them. But the body is an object as well as a subject: I can look at my hand lying on the table beside the paper.

The confusion starts when our knowledge of anatomy or physiology is superimposed on our direct bodily experience. Human anatomy and physiology are about the body, of which one's own body is a specimen. To study anatomy and physiology is to learn about the respiratory, circulatory and digestive systems, the autonomic and central nervous systems and brain, the skeletal structure, etc. One

B   3

learns that one has an oesophagus, two retinae with $6\frac{1}{2}$ million cones each, bronchial tubes, ductless glands, etc., just as one has skin and toenails, and that electrochemical impulses are conducted by the nerves – one's own nerves, for they are in one's own body, aren't they? – and so on. It is natural to think: " All that goes on in me ", for of course what one normally means by " me " is partly at least this body here, one's own body.

One thinks then of one's body in terms of anatomy, physiology, biochemistry, and even physics, and if one pleases as a system of systems of homeostatic or feedback mechanisms. It is simply a specimen of its kind. I could examine my own skin under the microscope, read my own E.E.G., just like anybody else's. Let us call the body in this sense the organism. No doubt the range of individual variation is in some respects very wide, but any two adult male organisms of an age, for example, are closely isomorphic in structure and function.

One arrives at this view by a natural development of ordinary realism, according to which the body is real in the sense that it can be seen and touched, just like the table or chair. Like all such things it has an inside, and the inside is as physiology and anatomy say it is. Just as there are tables and rocks, so there are organisms.

But if one's own body is an organism, one's bodily sensations, one's bodily experience, have to be occurrences in the organism, since they are in one's body. But this is not so: no such occurrences are describable in terms of the organism. Occurrences and processes in the organism are correlated with bodily sensations, but whereas these sensations are directly experienced, the occurrences in the organism, which are of extreme complexity, can only be discovered by elaborate experiment and inference. Sensations are in the body but not in the organism. The organism is entirely an object, an object for investigation and experiment.

What is investigated, however, is not one's own body in the primary sense. What is meant by the expression " my own body " is my embodiment. Whatever else I am, I am this body, and whatever else I mean by " I " I do mean my own body, whereby I am in a place, somewhere, situated. " Here " means " where I am bodily ". All my activities are conducted in or from the place where I am, and when

4

I move, I move bodily. There is a world for me primarily because I am always bodily situated in the midst of it.

What I see is seen from where I am. I see with my eyes, I move them, screw them up, try to see more with them. When I laugh, I laugh bodily; the laughter shakes me. When I talk, I talk with my throat, tongue, teeth and lips. When I am thinking, part of the time I am talking to myself, or making faces, or frowning, or curling my toes, or moving the pen across the paper, and these are not accessory, unconnected activities but all part of what I am at when I would say I was thinking. I am thinking bodily in a still more obvious way when I play to my opponent's weak backhand on the tennis court.

Though most of the time I am taking my body for granted and paying no attention to it, having habits and skills on which I count, it takes only a moment's reflection to describe some typical aspects of bodily experience, to say roughly what it means to be embodied, and what the expression "my own body" primarily means. What it does not mean in this sense is an organism. Like all human activities, the investigation of the organism is conducted by embodied selves. Hypothesis and theory remain idle till someone confirms or fails to confirm a prediction, and this is done almost always by seeing with his eyes.

A schoolbook on elementary physiology is called *How Your Body Works*. The distinction is simply not made in popular language. But it can be made very simply with reference to this title. How my body works in one sense is how I work, for I work bodily. But a book on that would tell me little or nothing. The title, however, obviously refers to the physiological on-goings in the organism, some of which can be correlated with my bodily experience and activity, my own body.

This distinction between the body and the organism is not a distinction between two entities, nor between a physical entity and its representation "in the mind". It is a distinction between the body as self or subject, and the body as object. The pain is in the subject but not in the object. The toothache can be in the upper jaw of the subject, the caries in a tooth on the lower jaw in the object. "Here" is where the subject is. The subject studies the organism with his eyes and hands, but up to a point he can regard his own body for this purpose as an object, measure his blood-pressure, test his reflexes, and many other things, as he might another body.

The distinction is not an easy one to make, for even in direct experience the body is to some extent an object – for instance one can see a good part of it, though always more or less from the same angle, unlike the other things about it. But in any sort of action or activity it is not an object but a subject – its movements are mine. In no sense is it true to say it *obeys* me – I am my own body. Volitions followed by bodily happenings belong to the domain of philosophical fiction. In action, the body is experienced as my power to do this and that. Things are seen as within reach of my arm, my arm is the power to reach them.

This essential ambiguity, as Merleau-Ponty calls it, of the body – whereby it is me, my own body, a subject, on the one hand, and an organism, an object, on the other – this essential ambiguity has led to endless confusion, and it is no doubt because many philosophers and others have found it intolerable that they have attempted to deny one aspect or the other. Most of them have chosen, subtly or crudely, to deny the body as subject, though in the nature of the case they could never quite succeed. To attempt this, they had to deny that experience, bodily experience, could really be as it obviously is, or attempt to maintain that it came to be as it obviously is from a genetic condition which would be consistent with their premises. This original experience was, like the state of nature, a myth. But it survives in attenuated form into the twentieth century. Why did most philosophers agree to regard the body as essentially an object, a thing in the world with all the other things? Natural philosophy, and above all Newtonian mechanics, had become the very type of genuine knowledge, of experimentally verifiable law. What other knowledge of the body could there be?

If this is the type of knowledge, my subjective bodily experience, the experience of seeing with my eyes, of walking, running, writing, reaching for, of carnal passion, can never be a matter of knowledge. Of any description of my embodiment, my bodily experience, it can be asked: How do you know this? How can this be verified? What is the proof? If knowledge is knowledge of the objective world, experimentally and publicly verifiable, there is no proof. The only evidence of seeing is to see, and the only evidence of the bodily experience of running, writing, etc., is to run, write, etc. I can improve in a literary way my description of bodily experience, make it more detailed and analytic, but to ask for verification of the kind in question is an absurdity. I can describe it carelessly. I can tell lies about it. But in the sense demanded I cannot verify it. For verification in the sense demanded always presupposes it.

Someone has to read the thermometer or the E.E.G., observe the explosion or the rat in the maze, and write down with his hand, or dictate with his tongue, teeth and lips, the results. If I ask him how he knows that what he describes *did* happen, his only answer can be " I saw it ". I know what he means, because I know what it is to see, to see with my own eyes. My embodiment in a sense is *a priori*: it is a condition of the possibility of objective knowledge, of knowledge of the organism – the body as object – as much as of anything else. Reference to bodily experience is part and parcel of the common language; it cannot be otherwise understood. It means what it does mean, because experience is as it is.

Behaviourism makes use of this common understanding of what it is to see, to be hungry, etc., but thinks to be " scientific " by never referring to it or by putting these words in quotation marks. Linguistic behaviourism in some of its forms purports to regard language solely as an autonomous domain of objective phenomena. Ryle's procedure, as I shall try to show, requires him to treat the self as another other. The problem of other selves and their embodied experience is thus dismissed: all selves are others and all others are objects. Ryle is saved in practice by his good sense, but his good sense is often at odds with what seems to be his philosophical doctrine.

In regarding the body simply as an object, philosophy was still left with the mind, and it was a disembodied mind. In earlier doctrines the soul at least inhabited or informed the body and moved it. The Cartesian doctrine of the body as a mechanism left nothing for the soul to do except think; the body would do what it did regardless, so long as it had a source of power and until the parts wore out. Descartes' physics required only configuration and motion, and his

7

physiology was derived from his physics, but what he called the fire-element, which in its pure form was the "animal spirits", fulfilled the rôle of a source of power. Descartes' theory of soul and body is complex and difficult and it continued to develop to the end of his life. Whether one takes it to be occasionalist, epiphenomenalist, or interactionist depends in part on what stage of its development is in question. There is no doubt, however, what interpretation was generally put upon the famous dualism, in spite of his insistence on the quasi-substantial unity of soul and body in ordinary experience – the body was purely a mechanism, whatever might be the nature of the soul.

In accounting for the occurrence of the ideas, Locke takes the mechanism for granted. But just as his doctrine of representative perception is largely ignored in practice, and his careful distinction of quality, sensation and idea abandoned, so his account of body and soul and consciousness is largely a straightforward, and admirable, account of ordinary experience in ordinary language, and the body in this context is certainly not a mechanism.

Bodily sensations were regarded by Locke's successors as the very type of "original" sensation. Berkeley in his youth was far more of a sensationalist than Locke, and if one regards, as one may, his mature doctrine as consisting essentially in verbal legislation, remained one to the end. For the original separation of all the ideas which together we call an apple could only be deduced from the separation of the external sense organs and some physiological theory. Colours and sounds were taken by Hume to be originally "of the nature" of sensation, like bodily pain. All the observable qualities of things which in the ordinary way we see in the things were "really" or "originally" sensations. Thus all experience must consist of sensations in various relations.

The doctrine was derived from physics and physiology. But the postulated atoms, of which bodily sensations were the pure type, were asserted to be given in experience, to be our immediate objects or data, or, since that might seem implausible, at least to have been so given "originally". Each of them was in itself independent of any other. But if this were so, all knowledge, all science, including physics and physiology, could be only of objects which were ultimately reducible to sensations in various relations. Part of the time, this was Hume's view. It followed that bodily sensations were not originally experienced as bodily, for the body like all other objects was reducible to sensations. Thus was the ladder kicked away.

Hume never entirely abandoned the physiological theory and often explicitly asserts it. But he confutes the representative theory to which it naturally leads, and is often essentially Berkeleyan. He saw that what he called Nature could only be what he perceived, imagined and believed. But he never frees himself from the metaphysics of natural philosophy. He is Newtonian, not only in his assumptions about the world, but in his approach to that domain of Nature which is human nature, whose nature it is to apprehend Nature in a certain way. In his ' official ' doctrine of association, nearly all our so-called knowledge is the mere effect of quasi-mechanical processes. " Nature, by an absolute uncontroulable necessity has determin'd us to judge as well as to breathe and feel." (*Treatise*, p. 183.) Probable reasoning, which for Hume comprises all empirical knowledge, is " nothing but a species of sensation" (*Treatise*, p. 103).

Hume means many things by " Nature ". He thinks of Nature as essentially beneficent, ensuring our well-being as it were in spite of us. He speaks of Nature as others speak of God, and this is more than merely the eighteenth-century habit of personification. Nature is Providence. But Nature is also the Nature of Newton's natural philosophy. Yet even in his strongly Newtonian introduction he writes: " All the sciences have a relation to human nature; and how-ever wide any of them seem to run from it, they still return back by one passage or another." (*Treatise*, p. xix.) But he can hardly have realised how far he would travel from his view of human nature as a part of Nature.

Nature, the natural world, he later concludes, consists of fictions of the imagination. Such, then, are the objects of Newtonian natural philosophy – but Hume does not say that. But the self is also a fiction, for all identities are fictions. Selves are not human nature but in a sense products or creations of human nature. They are among the constituted objects of the mind or consciousness, essentially assimilable,

9

when their identity is analysed, to other fictions constituted by the imagination and belief.

All nature, natural objects, objects of natural science, were constituted in this way. It is not difficult – in retrospect – to extract a doctrine of the transcendental, constitutive consciousness from Hume, but Husserl, so far as I am aware, was the first to do so. His tendency to subjective idealism was of course recognised. But in the forefront of the picture stands his doctrine of Nature, Nature the beneficent – made like God in Hume's own image – but also Newtonian Nature with its sub-domain human nature, the impressions and ideas and the quasi-mechanical principles of association. Hume is considered, and rightly considered, the forerunner of nineteenth-century sensationalism, psychologism, positivism, and, in a different way, introspectionism. Yet his doctrine of belief, imagination, and judgment which " peoples the world " (*Treatise*, p. 108) for all its inconsistencies and varieties of expression is distinctive and perhaps the most original thing in his whole work. The world as constituted by the imagination and belief has two intimately connected aspects: one is the system of memory and personal identity, and the other is the system of things in their causal relations. The essence of all the various fictions is identity in change. They are all ascribed to the imagination and belief. The imagination and belief, the constitutive consciousness, are not in nature, but are the correlate of nature. It is easy to go farther and say there is a world only for a consciousness.

Hume never said anything like this, but it is hard to avoid his invitation to say it. He has little to say about the faculties, propensities, dispositions and activities which he constantly and casually attributes to the mind, even as he develops his quasi-mechanical doctrine of association. He takes the mind for granted in much the same way as he takes Newtonian nature for granted when he is talking about the impressions and treats them in the Lockean fashion as the natural effects of physical causes. He both undermines the metaphysic of natural philosophy and continues to assume it. His analysis of causality makes it meaningless to ask the cause of the occurrence of impressions and ideas, for they, and they alone, are what we call causes and effects. There is no " double existence ", representing and represented (*Treatise*, p. 211).

Hume assigns a position of supreme importance to the science of man, " the only solid foundation for the other sciences ", even as he insists that he is applying " experimental philosophy " (the method of Newton) to " moral subjects ". " The essence of the mind is equally unknown with that of external bodies and it must be equally impossible to form any notion of its powers and qualities otherwise than by careful and exact experiments, and the observation of those particular effects, which result from its different circumstances and situations." (*Treatise*, pp. xx–xxi.)

This could be a programme for experimental psychology, for human as a branch of animal psychology, and Hume's short chapter, ' Of the Reason of Animals ', is in keeping with this view. But then there would be no ground at all for regarding the science of man as the only solid foundation for the other sciences. It would simply be one science among others. Whatever sense one gives to the word " foundation ", the relation of psychology and the social sciences to physics and chemistry cannot be so described. The problem of knowledge and of the relation of consciousness to its objects would remain untouched if the science of man were a science like any other science. Every psychology, however, leads to the problem of consciousness and thus beyond itself. Rats or other creatures may be described entirely in terms of their movements, however artificially, but unless I observe them and note what happens no experiment has been made. It is only because I believe that others actually see (are conscious) too that I accept numerous experimental findings which I have not myself made. The seeing or observing is not part of the experimental finding: only what is seen and observed is that. The seeing or observing are subjective: what is seen or observed is objective. But without seeing, nothing would be seen, no observation would be made, and no hypothesis tested.

CHAPTER TWO

IMPRESSIONS AND IDEAS

HUME'S emphasis on experiment means that he is going to stick to the evidence and not go beyond it. He will not impose " conjectures and hypotheses on the world for the most certain principles " (*Treatise*, p. xxii). It is because the doctrine of impressions and ideas is not regarded as a hypothesis but self-evident, that it is never fully formulated and always remains radically obscure and ambiguous. For the sensation doctrine, as we shall see, is not its only source. No less important for his doctrine of complex impressions and ideas is the mental image which is " in the mind " but not in the world and to which the complex impression is also assimilated as an " internal and perishing existence " (*Treatise*, p. 194). The mental image is hypostatised, as it so often is, as an intra-mental entity, and the complex impression is simply the more forceful and vivacious original of it, but none the less an intra-mental entity itself. This is what Sartre calls the illusion of immanence, the belief that the objects of consciousness are in consciousness, in the mind, as if the mind were a container. The use of the word " contents " in this connection probably derives from it.

The simple impressions of sensation, though they have a curious bearing on Hume's doctrine of mathematics and crop up from time to time in other contexts, may largely be neglected for my purpose. But they are important in one respect. They are simples, without parts, extensionless, or in other terms *minima sensibilia*. All complexes are mere sums of simples: a whole is the sum and nothing but the sum of its parts. In any given complex, the simples are finite in number. Divisibility is not infinite. It follows that any impression or idea is determinate in quantity as well as quality, since it consists of a definite number of simples. The only importance this doctrine has is that, though Hume perfectly well recognises that determination of quantity is not accomplished by counting the simples but by measurement according to a practical standard, he continues to assume that ideas or mental images, no less than the impressions of which they are copies, have a definite size. What he does not realise is that neither impressions nor ideas as such can be measured at all, and that it is absurd to assert that they are determinate in quantity if the quantity is in principle indeterminable. The height of a man can be measured but not the height of the mental image of the man, though the image be of a man of that height.

There is a further complication in the doctrine of impressions which is closely connected with the hypostatisation of the image. Though Hume frequently identifies impressions with qualities or properties of things in the same way as Locke and Berkeley – colour, taste, smell, texture, visual and tactual shape – he is convinced for much the same physiological reasons as Berkeley that " our sight informs us not of outness ", i.e. that any visual impression is in two dimensions, or at least " originally " in two dimensions. (*Treatise*, p. 191) It is a flat patchwork of colours. Hence that impression which would correspond, for example, to the appearance of the side of a house in the field of vision is held to be determinate in size. This view leads to what I call the illusion of real appearances. For any appearance of the house is simply the way it there looks to me here, the way I see it. But Hume's doctrine of the visual impression hypostatises the *look* of the house and holds that *this* is determinate in quantity or size. But, as I shall argue, only the house can be measured in any way and only it can be said to be of determinate size in any dimension.

Hume's theory of impressions and ideas is not like some sense-datum theories which purport to be just another way of talking about what in the ordinary way we say we see or hear or feel, and which are to be justified simply by their convenience, utility and unambiguousness. For Hume, we believe we see things, bodies, material existents. But these are not what is given. We take our perceptions to be our only objects, " and suppose, that the very being, which is intimately present to the mind, is the real body or material existence" (*Treatise*, p. 206). The bodies and the impressions are the same: the bodies are simply what we believe the impressions to be, but there is nothing but the impressions.

Yet Hume maintains paradoxically that " all sensations are felt by the mind, such as they really are, and that when we doubt, whether they present themselves as distinct objects, or as mere impressions, the difficulty is not concerning their nature, but concerning their relations and situation" (*Treatise*, p. 189).

I say " paradoxically " for we obviously do not feel them as they really are; we take them for bodies. Again Hume states:

> For since all actions and sensations of the mind are known to us by consciousness, they must necessarily appear in every particular what they are, and be what they appear. Every thing that enters the mind, being in *reality* a perception, 'tis impossible anything should to *feeling* appear different. This were to suppose, that even where we are most intimately conscious, we might be mistaken.
>
> (*Treatise*, p. 190)

The common injunction not to take Hume too literally is a bad one. It is not his expression but his doctrine that is difficult. In these passages, the difficulty is of a fundamental nature. If sensations were felt as they really are, how would the vulgar ever take them for external bodies? By reason of " their relations and situation ". Sensations are what they are and what they appear, irrespective of their relations to other sensations. Relations are purely external. But the vulgar are not conscious of some of their sensations as such; they suppose them to be bodies, and in this they are, in a sense, mistaken. The sensations as they really are are " known to us by consciousness ". Consciousness in this context must, I think, be the reflexive consciousness, and Hume seems to be asserting in Cartesian fashion that it is certain and indubitable.

What Hume is doing is alleging the evidence of our direct, intimate consciousness in favour of his doctrine of impressions and ideas. He identifies the sensation with what the vulgar take to be the objectively real qualities of bodies or material existents. Whereas, as he alleges, the vulgar take their perceptions to be their only objects, he takes what, for example, the vulgar call the colour of a thing to be a sensation of which we are most intimately conscious and about which we cannot be mistaken. Such a sensation is what it is and what it appears to be. It is a determinate colour, and it is nothing but a colour. It is a pure quality and it is presented as such, irrespective of its relations. Where does he get these pure sensations or qualities? They are simply the abstracted qualities of things. Anything may be analysed without remainder into its qualities. Those abstracted qualities he identifies with what he insists are the presented or felt sensations, of which we are most intimately conscious and about which we cannot be mistaken. The problem then concerns their relations and situation, that is, how these qualities or sensations are supposed jointly to compose a body or material existence.

The doctrine of impressions and ideas can only be understood historically as the late and sophisticated product of two centuries of physical, physiological and philosophical theory. To cite the evidence of our intimate consciousness is pure sleight of hand. What we are alleged to be intimately conscious of is actually deduced from this elaborate body of theory. It is perhaps unduly to rationalise Hume's position to say that he persuaded himself that what *must*, according to the theory, be presented to consciousness, *was* presented to consciousness. The difficulty was that the vulgar did not know it: they thought their sensations were qualities of bodies – the grass was green, the sky was blue, the sack heavy, the ditch foul-smelling.

This being so, Hume, try as he might to stick to the direct evidence, had to fall back on the scientific premises of the doctrine, though without always realising what he was doing. He had to say that " colours, sounds, etc., are originally on the same footing with the pain that arises from steel, and pleasure that proceeds from a fire " (*Treatise*, p. 192), where the meaning of " originally " is clearly " when we first have them ". The evidence for this could not be direct. It could only be in terms of the theory from which the doctrine originated.

But the physical theory took the physical world for granted, and it was the belief in the independent existence of body, of the physical world, which Hume undertook to account for on the basis of the alleged data. Not only were the data deduced from the physical theory: they were no longer data, for what the vulgar saw was not, for example, the pure quality red, but red in a perceptual context, for example, an attractive shiny red surface over there and *out* there. For Hume, there was the pure quality red; the " shininess " would have to be analysed as streaks of white as if what was presented were a painting; and the attractiveness was a sensation of pleasure caused by the impression of sensation and projected upon it. There would be absolutely no intrinsic connection between the red and the white and the pleasure as they might be supposed to have occurred separately, originally. Hume's theory was to account for experience as we actually have it, for, that is, the vulgar consciousness, on the premise that what was given were sensations.

It followed from the doctrine of impressions or sensations that the senses were the faculty of receiving, or apprehending, or just having sensations, nothing less and nothing more. This concept of the senses is no less far removed from actual experience than is the concept of a sensation, of which it is the strict correlative. Our actual sense-experience consists not simply of passive bodily sensations, but of looking, listening, touching, handling. The pure sensing of the sensations is at best a hypothesis, but there is no evidence for it in experience; the " evidence " is that of the external sense organs which receive and transmit impressions, according to the then theory. Whenever Hume wants to appeal in a concrete way to the reader's experience it is never to his experience of impressions and ideas as *such* that he appeals, for obvious reasons. And when Hume introduces the distinction between impressions and ideas, in order to say what he means at all, he has in effect to treat impressions as identical with material existences, independently existing, or with observable qualities of such things. He thus puts the alleged vulgar belief in reverse: the vulgar take their perceptions to be their only objects; Hume takes the objects to be his perceptions.

We shall " readily perceive " the difference between the impression and the idea, he confidently asserts. We do readily perceive it because the distinction he makes is that between seeing and imagining material existences.

When I shut my eyes and think of my chamber, the ideas I form are exact representations of the impressions I felt; nor is there any circumstance of the one, which is not to be found in the other ... I can imagine to myself such a city as the *New Jerusalem* ... tho' I never saw any such. I have seen *Paris*; but shall I affirm I can form such an idea of that city, as will perfectly represent all its streets and houses in their real and just proportions?

(Treatise, p. 3)

CHAPTER THREE

SEEING AND IMAGINING

If we did not see things and imagine things we should never know what Hume meant by his distinction between an impression and an idea. But in a sense we still do not know – we know what the distinction corresponds to but we do not know what is meant by an impression or an idea. The only way to show that we have impressions and ideas, or that there are impressions and ideas, would be to start from the vulgar consciousness and indicate that feature or element of what we experience which would be called an impression or idea. Any fruitful analysis of sense-experience should start from sense-experience, not from physics or physiology or what else we have learned about the world by means of sense-experience, nor from the observed behaviour of rats or monkeys or infants. Actual sense-experience as we have it could never be deduced from any such evidence – all such evidence presupposes and depends upon our own sense-experience. To say this is also to say that the attempt to identify pure data, the immediate data of consciousness, is futile and nugatory. If there were a pure datum of consciousness we should be conscious of it: it would be actually given to consciousness. All alleged data prove to be merely identifiable elements or features or characteristics of things, products of analysis.

The method I shall use is that of reflexive analysis. Any description of experience, and not merely of what we experience, is reflexive. A description of a table would not be a description of experience; but a description of seeing a table would be. In other words, such a description would not merely describe something, an object, in the world, but the way in which one is conscious of it. Seeing, for example, is not reducible to what is seen, though it is inseparable from it. It is the subjective correlate of what is visible. But for reflexion I could not meaningfully say that I see anything. Reflexion is commonplace and indispensable, and any kind of waking consciousness or experience may become reflexive. (I am inclined to think that to reflect while dreaming is to wake up.) What is frequently meant by " consciousness " is the reflexive consciousness, and this is one reason why the term is so ambiguous – though not nearly so ambiguous as " unconscious ". But consciousness or experience need not be reflexive. I can be absorbed in a task and all my attention can be devoted to what I am at. I am of course seeing what is before me all the time, but it is it and not the seeing that occupies me. But my seeing it is implicit in its visibility, its being seen, and I can make this explicit and be aware of seeing it. It is not the seeing alone that I am aware of in reflexion, for there is no seeing without something seen. What I am reflexively aware of is my seeing something.

Phenomenology is reflexive description and analysis. It is not description and analysis of any objective aspect of the world, but of our experience of the world. No general account of phenomenological analysis can do more than provide preliminary orientation. The proof of the pudding is in the eating. I should say a word about the Husserlian ἐποχή, the putting in parenthesis or suspension of the natural attitude and the natural thesis of the world, the assumption that there is a world, Hume's natural belief. This attitude or thesis is not suspended, for it cannot be suspended. But it is itself analysed reflexively. As I shall show, the analysis of seeing and imagining cannot be made except in relation to the natural thesis of the world, nor could any distinction be established between seeing and imagining. Sense-experience is inseparable from the natural thesis of the world, Hume's vulgar consciousness. There is no sort of sense-experience other than that of the vulgar consciousness.

Sense-experience is experience of things in the world, one world, by different senses. We do not construct one object or one world out of correlated data supplied by different senses. Our experience is of touching and smelling the very table which we see; the same table is touched, seen and smelt. The vulgar consciousness or the natural attitude are not only vulgar and natural but provide, overtly or covertly, the basis for all arguments which criticise them or hold them to be in any sense unwarranted. It is not possible not to believe in the visible, tangible, spatio-temporal world. Evidence is of this or that, what is or is not the case, what there is and what there is not, but the thesis of the world is independent of any particular fact or any particular existent – it is *in the world* that what is or is not the case is ascertained. That any fact can be found out and established presupposes a world.

To attempt to make the distinction between seeing and imagining without reference to things in the world is impossible. To attempt this is to attempt to analyse experience while trying to ignore actual experience. That is why the only feasible sense-datum theory would be simply another way of talking about things in the world, except that one could not talk, as Ayer virtually shows in *The Foundations of Empirical Knowledge*.

Hume's distinction between impressions and ideas is made in terms of their force and vivacity. If an idea were forceful and vivacious enough it would be an impression. (Hume's mechanism of sympathy depends upon this principle whereby an idea can actually become an impression.) He illustrates the difference by means of the difference between seeing and imagining his chamber. But the difference does not lie in the force or vivacity of the chamber, which may be brightly or dimly lit, smoky or clear. Furthermore we can see it unobservantly, abstractedly, without taking any special notice of it, and we can imagine it vividly and in detail. But to imagine it vividly is not to see it, and to see it apathetically is not to imagine it.

The chamber being granted, however, the distinction is easy to make. We can only see it or part of it when we are bodily in it and looking with our eyes open. We can, if we will, examine it in more detail, discovering more and more. It is revealed; we do not invent it. We need not wonder what some detail is like: we look, and it is revealed in its unpredictable particularity. When we imagine it, we do not need to be bodily in it, and if we are, it is easier to imagine it with the eyes shut. We can never discover anything about the chamber this way, though we may try to remember more detail. There is a limit to what we can imagine with any confidence that we are imagining it as it is, i.e. as we would see it to be if we were actually in it and looking round it. We can at will imagine it as other than it is, and cannot be certain that some particulars we imagine are such as it really has. If someone asks us questions of detail about it, there are some we cannot answer. We can always give an answer, but it can be wrong. The only way to know is to go to the chamber and look.

To make this distinction with reference to the chamber is to make it in the only possible way. In the natural attitude there is a world of visible, tangible things which we can and do see and touch directly. We are in the midst of it, wherever we happen to be, being ourselves embodied, and we see what we see from where we are with our eyes. To see is to have direct access to the things in the world, to find what is there and not invent it. It is all there already, even when we can't make out what we want to make out, when we can't see it properly. We know what to do when we can't see anything properly – we must get close enough; then if the light is good enough we'll see it, or if not, we can try to touch it, feel what it is like. Some things we see will not yield to this treatment: we cannot see more of a rainbow or mirage by getting closer. We can see where the rainbow ends, but only from another place, not from where it ends. Even so, we have discovered something about the world – that is the way rainbows are, and how else should we discover this but by seeing, by going and looking?

The things that we have got to know by seeing how they are, we can imagine as we saw them, but we can also imagine them as other than we saw them, as changed. And we can never be certain that they were as we now imagine them, nor that they are now as they were when we saw them: to know that, we would have to see the things themselves again. But if they are still there at all, they are as they are, there to be looked at, if we could get within sight of them, and if they are not there at all now, there will be something else there anyway. By the thesis of the world, we are where we are in it and can only see so much from where we are, but imagine whatever we please. Without positing things in the world, no distinction can be made, for to see something is to see something which is there to be seen, visible. The seeing and the thing itself are inseparable. This point is often made about the primary meaning of the verb ' to see '. One cannot be said literally to see something which does not exist and which is not there within one's range of vision.

When we imagine something we may posit it as existing elsewhere, as absent, as not existing at all, or as " neutral " when we do not posit it either as existing or as not existing. (Cf. Sartre, *L'Imaginaire*, p. 35.) In any case it is not bodily, visibly, tangibly present, to be explored and discovered and examined. Imagining is a way of making quasi-present what it posited as being absent. One of the difficulties about Hume's analysis of this in terms of natural belief is that though it covers the case of imagining something which we posit as existing elsewhere in the world, it does not cover the case of imagining, say, a purely imaginary building, which is yet imagined as a building – an object of belief and not simply a complex idea.

Leave the actual things in the world out of account, and this whole distinction between seeing and imagining collapses. But Hume's distinction between impressions and ideas depends entirely on this familiar distinction. There have to be things, real things, in order to make it. But what we call a thing independently existing is not simply a complex impression or idea, for these are " internal and perishing existences ", as he later calls them. They are " in the soul ", not in the world. It is for this reason that Hume does not elaborate the distinction between seeing his chamber and imagining it, for though his distinction is entirely parasitic on this one, he does not mean to bring the chamber into it at all. Hence his distinction between the impressions and ideas is made in terms of the vague and unsatisfactory force and vivacity. The chamber is an identity and all identities are fictions based upon our "broken" but resembling perceptions. The distinction between the impressions and ideas is supposed to be made independently of the fictions, for it forms an essential part of his account of the creation of the fictions.

Hume never gives examples of impressions or ideas as such. Not only in the early sections but throughout the book, all his examples are of things in the world – mountains, houses, trees, his chamber, table, books. He has no choice, for to speak meaningfully he must speak of the things which we see or imagine. But when he speaks of impressions and ideas without giving any examples, then they are not things in the world. Nor are they always merely intra-mental objects – they are often both objects and the consciousness of them. This ambiguity is inherent in his use of the term " perception " which can mean the perceiving or the perceived or both at once. In the last case, the consciousness of the object and the object of consciousness are identified. This is one of the sources of the illusion of real appearances and of the hypostatised image.

CHAPTER FOUR

THE ILLUSION OF
IMMANENCE [1]

WHAT leads Hume to treat impressions and ideas as things when he is giving illustrations but as internal and perishing existences when he is not? Both impressions and ideas are called perceptions and there is no hard and fast distinction between them. An idea corresponds to what is now called a mental image. It is easy to regard a mental image as some sort of entity. But it obviously is not in the world like a table or a chair or even a mirage or a rainbow. It is spatial if it is visual, but it isn't one of the things in the common space, spatially related to all the other things in the world. It is not situated anywhere. But it is an image, isn't it? It must be somewhere, mustn't it? But not in the world. In the mind? Well, the mind is not of course a place, but there are minds, aren't there? So it must be in the mind, an intramental object, an internal and perishing existence.

Images come and go, the argument might continue, and when they go they are no more, they do not exist. They are exactly as they appear – there is no more to them than appears, than we are aware of. We are aware of a mental image or there is no mental image, and we are entirely aware of all of it. Hume *partly* recognised this essential point, which others have sometimes failed to recognise – there is no more to the image than one actually imagines. One can go on describing what it is of and imagining more and more of that – the characteristics of the thing – and a natural illusion for those who regard an image as a picture is to suppose that it is the image they are describing, and that there is more in it than they happen to notice at any time.

[1] This chapter is based upon the analysis in the first part of *L'Imaginaire* which Sartre optimistically calls ' Le Certain '.

But " in " the image there is nothing that one is not, *as it were*, noticing. How could there be? It would literally be a thing or a picture then; one would be seeing it.

We cannot be mistaken about anything in it, for " this were to suppose that even where we are most intimately conscious, we might be mistaken ". We can make mistakes about things; we cannot make mistakes about mental images – they are, one might think, exactly as they appear. But they are very like what we see. They can be quite detailed. Exact copies, one might say. But fainter, sketchier. Hence, they differ only in force and vivacity, " not in nature ". And as an idea or mental image is an object, but only an intramental object, an internal and perishing existence, so is an impression: it is just more forceful and vivacious: " whatever is true of the one must be acknowledg'd concerning the other." (*Treatise*, p. 19.)

When Hume speaks of them as objects, though he uses the word in more than one sense, he is not necessarily confusing them with things in the world (objects of belief), for he does indeed regard them as the immediate given objects of consciousness, and in a sense the only objects, which, however, we take to be external, continuing existences, things in the world. But it is not only by reason of the language that, in giving examples, he has to refer to things in the world. The fundamental reason is that an idea or image is always an idea or image *of* something, whether the something actually exists or does not exist, whether it is a fiction or a mere possibility or a reality. That is why he has to talk in the way he does about ideas *of* such-and-such.

" I have seen Paris; but shall I affirm I can form such an idea of that city, as will perfectly represent all its streets and houses in their real and just proportions? " (*Treatise*, p. 3.) Hume is here talking in the natural way, according to the thesis of the world, describing what it is to see and what to imagine Paris. But on his view of impressions and ideas he has no right to be doing this, for an impression simply is what it is and what it appears to be, and so is an idea; they are objects in the mind, not in the world. In what sense could they be *of* anything? They would have to be representations of it, and this Hume emphatically rejects; there is no double existence, representing and represented.

It may be asked how we can know that ideas are copies of impressions. Hume acknowledges that it is "impossible to recall the past impressions, in order to compare them with our present ideas" (*Treatise*, p. 85). But he never explains how, if we cannot recall past impressions, we can know we have had past impressions, for the idea "of memory" is simply a present idea, distinguished from the idea of imagination by its force and vivacity. (See Chapter 13, in which I examine Russell's similar account of memory.)

But Hume recognises that an impression or idea cannot strictly be of anything: "To form the idea of an object, and to form an idea simply is *the same thing*: the reference of the idea to an object being an extraneous denomination, of which in itself it bears no mark or character." (*Treatise*, p. 20.) It is like a picture *of* a landscape, which is just a patchwork of colours on canvas. His account of the "idea of existence" follows accordingly:

> There is no impression or idea of any kind, of which we have any consciousness or memory, that is not conceived as existent; and 'tis evident, that from this consciousness the most perfect idea and assurance of *being* is derived. . . . The idea of existence, then, is the very same with the idea of what we conceive to be existent. To reflect on anything simply, and to reflect on it as existent, are nothing different from each other. That idea, when conjoined with the idea of an object, makes no addition to it. Whatever we conceive, we conceive to be existent. Any idea we please to form is the idea of a being; and the idea of a being is any idea we please to form.
>
> (*Treatise*, pp. 66–7)

What exists is impressions and ideas and nothing else. The idea of an object and the idea *as* an object – the idea-object – are the same thing: the idea is itself the object and the only object. That is the theory which all his examples confound.

The things in the world, his chamber, mountains, trees, the buildings and streets of Paris, all that in the ordinary way we say exists, are objects of belief, i.e. ideas enlivened by belief or assent. But all ideas in Hume's terms exist, and it is not in point of existence that one idea differs from another. His problem remains unsolved: how we can have an image *of* anything when the image *is* it. What I image has its place in the world; it is not my image, though I believe it exists; my image is *of* it, or in other words, I am imaging *it*. Not for a moment do I take my image of the Pan Am building for the Pan Am building. But that is certainly what I am imaging; I mean that very building in New York; it is of *it* that I have an image. It does not help Hume in the slightest to say that the reference of an idea to an object is an extraneous denomination; no such reference would be possible on his theory. On his theory, you could not imagine the buildings of Paris, for your present lively ideas, enlivened by belief, would *be* the buildings of Paris. Your enlivened image would be not *of* them, but *them*. But the evidence of reflexion is decisive: when I image the streets of Paris, and when I imagine myself there, the thesis of the world is effective, and what I mean is that very city 4000 miles away, not my image. The image is not an entity. When I (here) imagine Paris (there), I am said to be having an image, but this is only one way of talking. If an image were a picture it could be looked at, but one can never look at it; all one can do is to imagine more.

Hume's doctrine of impressions and ideas has its source in the theory of sensation.

> 'Tis certain, that the mind, in its perceptions, must begin some-where; and that since the impressions precede their correspondent ideas, there must be some impressions, which without any intro-duction make their appearance in the soul. As they depend upon natural and physical causes, the examination of them wou'd lead me too far from my present subject, into the sciences of anatomy and natural philosophy.
>
> (*Treatise*, p. 275)

The complex impression " as it makes its appearance in the soul " is assimilated to the mental image; it is simply more forceful and vivid. If one regards the mental image as an intra-mental entity or object, it is easy to regard what it is of as being that which it resembles, of which it is a copy, and hence to regard this original as being also an intra-mental entity, an internal and perishing existence. An impression, then, is just a lively mental image.

The ordinary distinction between seeing (or touching or hearing) and imagining, according to which an identical object can be seen or imagined, is a distinction between two types of consciousness of an object, two ways of " intending " it, of having it in mind. Hume, however, puts the distinction into the substitute intra-mental objects. I can see St Paul's or I can imagine St Paul's. For Hume, in the first case there is a lively object, and in the second case a less lively one which is like it. (How it could be known to be like it, Hume never explains.) There are two objects, not one: what is called seeing goes into the one, and what is called imaging or imagining goes into the other. But though Hume in this way identifies the object of consciousness and the consciousness of the object, as the very word " perception " in his usage implies, he also retains a mind or consciousness which is not identified with the object, and in terms of which the distinction between seeing and imagining is also made. He has thus two parallel distinctions: (a) in terms of the force and vivacity of the object, and (b) in terms of the liveliness with which we apprehend it, the manner of our apprehension (*Treatise*, p. 96).

Hume, as I have said, takes the mind for granted, even when he is reducing personal identity to " nothing but a bundle or collection of different perceptions ". The propensities, dispositions, activities, and operations of the mind are repeatedly invoked. How these are to be reconciled with the quasi-mechanical principles of association, whereby Hume attempts to account for as much of experience as he possibly can, is nowhere explained. Where the principles of association are employed, the mind – if there were a mind – would be a purely passive, receptive, contemplative consciousness. Even the passions – the impressions of reflexion – when regarded from this point of view would occur to an essentially unmoved unimpassioned consciousness. But it is evident that Hume does not always conceive the mind in this way. It has " command over all its ideas " (*Treatise*, p. 624), it is enlivened by an impression and " enlivens " an idea. And identity is the product of the imagination. But Hume expounds no theory of the mind or consciousness, but only of the intra-mental objects and the objects of belief, the fictitious identities of the imagination.

This is one of the most important sources of ambiguity in Hume's theory; the object of consciousness and the consciousness of the object are identified in the perception, but there is still a mind or consciousness left over of which the perception is an object. It is entirely uncertain whether Hume recognised any distinction between a lively idea and the lively apprehension of an idea. At any rate, he treats them as interchangeable and this is perfectly natural. To apprehend something in a lively manner is to apprehend something lively. The intentional act or noesis and the intentional object or noema correspond. But Hume never actually makes this point, and it would be far-fetched to extract a doctrine of intentionality from his work. It would be completely at odds with his doctrine of impressions and ideas and the principles of association, and with his view of the mental image as an entity or intra-mental object, a sort of picture having no essential relations to whatever it might be thought to picture.

Hume's description of any idea or image is in effect a description of a thing in the world, which he assumes in the commonsense way to be fully determinate, and just as the thing can be reduced to the sum of its abstracted qualities and dimensions, so also can the image – it is nothing but its " pure " qualities and these are the immediate data of consciousness. One cannot be in error about these; they are entirely as they appear. He never ceases to identify the determinate, objective qualities of things with what is immediately given in direct experience, for the things in the world, the fictions, are entirely reducible to the immediate data.

Some qualities, such as visible shape and colour, which are obviously not the same quality, raise a serious problem for Hume, for they cannot be regarded as separate impressions. Flying in the face of his distinction between them, he insists that what is not separable is not distinguishable, and then goes on to show that it is – by means of comparison of things alike in colour but not in shape, or alike in shape but not in colour. He simply contradicts himself, for what is not separable in this case, quite plainly *is* distinguishable. Why does he insist again and again that what is not separable is not distinguishable? He identifies what is given with the qualities of things in the world, regardless of the fact that these different qualities are singled out or abstracted in predication and are not *given*, each of them, so to speak, on its own on a plate. Two of these qualities are obviously shape and colour, but no less obviously there can be no impression of uncoloured shape nor of unshaped colour. So there cannot be any distinction. But there is. Having denied it, he has to make it (*Treatise*, p. 25). Hume would never land himself in such a position if he did not have to. He had to do so, because he always assumed with Berkeley that what was given were the qualities of things, and these he identified with the impressions. But, if I may repeat the point yet again, whenever he takes an example of an impression or idea or describes one, it is a thing he refers to and describes. But sometimes he also means an appearance of a thing, and of this I shall have more to say, for as I shall show it is far more plausible in some respects to identify the mental image as a copy of an appearance of a thing, than as a copy of a thing.

But first, the mental image itself, which is his fundamental model. It is regarded as an intra-mental object. But if one asks how one mental image is distinguished from another or how it is identified, the answer has to be in terms of what it is of. This applies no less to the purely imaginary than to images of existing things or people. The distinction between an image of Lyndon B. Johnson and an image of Dean Rusk is the distinction between L. B. J. and Dean Rusk. If one asks how high an image of L. B. J. is, there is no answer, for it is only things in the common space that have a measurable and determinable height, breadth or depth. An image of L.B.J. is " spatial ", but it has no height for it is not in space. The space is a quasi-space and the height a quasi-height. So also for the temporal characteristic. An image of L. B. J. at the Democratic Convention in August 1964 is not in August 1964, nor is a bodily image of the heat in the hall. The time of the image is a quasi-time. The questions " when? ", " where? ", " how tall? " and so on can only be asked of what the image is of. There is no difficulty in saying or guessing the dimensions and the date of what I am imaging – these are *the* date and dimensions, which one may read about in the newspapers. I may get the date wrong or the dimensions wrong, but for them to be wrong there must be the correct date and dimensions. But the image has none – it is " quasi- " through and through. One cannot be wrong or right about its dimensions. To image a small thing and image a huge thing is not to have a small image and a huge image. The difference is in the things. The image, as Sartre says, is a consciousness of ——, an imaging, an imaging consciousness, and since it is just an imaging there is nothing " in " the image but what one actually images. Hence it cannot be examined and scrutinised as a picture can be, for there is nothing to scrutinise or examine.

One cannot ask how distant the image is; for there is no answer to the question " distant from what ?" In an image of someone at a distance the distance is imaged like everything else; one can have an image of L. B. J. at fifty yards, but not an image at fifty yards of L. B. J. If it is an image of a picture of L. B. J., it is an image of a picture at six feet, for example, not an image at six feet of a picture, not a picture of a picture. It is of course partly because pictures, which are things, are also usually of things, that mental images are regarded as a kind of picture: to image something is to picture it, to quasi-see it. And indeed the fact that pictures, sculptures and models are of things probably underlies all doctrines which make the object of consciousness a representation of something, including of course the doctrine of representative perception.

The only reason for making a distinction between imaging and imagining in this context is that one can image, for example, someone's face nowhere in particular, at no particular distance and in no particular situation, but one can also imagine him sitting in a chair across the room talking and oneself sitting at a certain distance from him. That is to say one imagines a situation with oneself in it looking at someone else. In making up a story, one imagines also the situation in a wider sense: the scene imaged gets its significance from this. In imaging someone at some distance, the imagined situation generally includes oneself, the imaged " over there " is in relation to the imagined " here ". One imagines oneself bodily in a certain situation, though as in seeing something from a certain position, the consciousness of one's own body is implicit, or non-thetic. (Cf. *L'Imaginaire*, p. 23.) Imagining a situation and imagining that something is the case can amount to the same thing. " Imagining " of course has other meanings too; it can, for example, mean " believing falsely ". But that does not really affect this analysis.

One need not, however, imagine any situation or context or place in order to image someone or something, or to image a smell or taste or " feel " or a bodily sensation. One can image someone's expression without imaging any feature of his face clearly: one may be quite unable to recall the colour of his eyes, for example, or what his teeth are like though one is imaging him with a broad grin. Mental images are not " determinate in quality and quantity ". Furthermore, vividness may be entirely independent of detail, being essentially affective, as I shall try to show at a later stage.

Whether one is seeing L. B. J. or imaging L. B. J. it is the same man that one is seeing or imaging. If it were any sort of simulacrum or picture that one had before one in imaging, how would one know it was a simulacrum or of whom it was a simulacrum? To know this one would have to remember the original, and to remember the original would be just to have that or another simulacrum. This is essentially the difficulty that Hume is in when he asserts that ideas are copies of impressions. The answer to the question " what are you imagining? " or " what is your image of? " is not simply determined by the form of the question. If one is imaging a certain person it could not be anyone or anything but that very person one is imaging. Only the view of the image as a mental occurrence, a mental picture or scene on the stage of one's inner theatre which one introspects could have led people to suppose otherwise. One means the very person one images, and that person is certainly not in person on any stage " in one's mind ". That person may not be where one imagines him and of course, in the case of a memory image, not at the time one imagines him. He may be dead though one imagines him alive or as he was when alive. But the image is not an occurrence independent of the meant identity, the object or person, which is imaged. That is Hume's theory, and later Russell's theory; the identity is a construction out of intra-mental occurrences.

Reflexion refutes this view: imaging presupposes the identity of the thing or person imaged. The positing of the object as existing elsewhere, as absent, as no longer existing, as non-existent, as possible or " neutral " is essential. To image a dragon, to imagine a situation that might have been but was not, or is not yet but may be, is to posit them as non-existent or not having been or yet to be. That is to say, one assumes the world in which some things are and some things aren't, some things and events have been, have happened, and some things haven't. One's true beliefs and one's false beliefs equally pre-suppose the world, which is as it is, independently of what one believes. The thesis of the world is that the world is as one knows it but there is much more to it than one knows. All that one imagines or images assumes the world, and the thesis of the world is based above all on our being bodily in the midst of it, inhabiting it. To be in the world is to be situated in relation to what else there is or was, near or remote in time or space.

A theory which, like Hume's, takes a mental image to be an entity, hypostatises a kind of consciousness of things, and makes this hypostasis what we are conscious of. But what we are conscious of is simply what we imagine – the thing or person or situation. There are no intra-mental entities; all there is is in the world.

To remember or recall is to be conscious of what is past. But in the Humean and similar later theories one cannot literally do this, for what is past is no more and whatever one is conscious of must be present now. Pastness has therefore to be, or be reducible to, some characteristic of what is present; the passage of time has, as it were, to be represented by dates stamped on what is present. The " present " itself becomes an entirely nugatory concept. One is forced into such a view if one assumes that what one is conscious of, the object of consciousness, what one sees or imagines, is *in* consciousness, in the mind, an intra-mental entity. But what one is remembering, thinking of, imagining, does not need to be now any more than it needs to be here. In any case, these words have no meaning except in relation to " then " and " there ". There is only one answer to the question, what I am imagining, when I imagine my flat in Edinburgh, and only one answer to the question, what I am remembering, when I recall a party in it four years ago. If I were not here now, it would not be there and " ago ", as I think of it.

One need never speak of mental images at all. I suspect that the expression is inherited from introspectionist psychology and philosophy, according to which there were two domains in which events occurred and could be observed: the world and the mind. The natural way of talking is to say one imagines something or recalls something. But the view that when one " has an image " one is contemplating an intra-mental entity is deeply rooted. When one denies this, one is often taken to be denying that people have mental images. One man, for example, will assert emphatically that in doing a calculation he reads the answer off the slide rule in his head. This is not only a legitimate use of the English language; it is an excellent description. But there is no slide rule in his head, nor is he literally reading off the slide rule. He is imagining the slide rule, the setting, and what it would read. This is a perfectly normal way of doing mental calculations; some people imagine a blackboard. To think in images is not to contemplate or look at intra-mental entities.

CHAPTER FIVE

THE ILLUSION OF
REAL APPEARANCES

THE impressions that Hume has in mind are for the most part visual,
and such an impression has to be thought of as a flat patchwork of
colours at no distance. Owing to his constant reference to things,
impressions are also identifiable with qualities of things, e.g. the redness
and shine of an apple, and there is no doubt that Hume thought of
them in this way quite often. But strictly, as he makes plain when he
insists that " our sight informs us not of outness ", the visual impression
is a flat patchwork. What it corresponds to is the visual field or,
more narrowly, to one appearance of a thing in the visual field. It is
" determinate in quality and quantity " (*Treatise*, p. 19), not only of a
definite colour but of a definite size, and shape.

The mistake which he makes is not confined to those who have held
that our sight informs us not of outness. It is simply the belief that the
size and shape of an appearance of a thing are determinate or determinable. Once again the trouble arises from, or is at least accentuated by,
regarding an appearance as if it were a picture, and the camera has
if anything tended to confirm the illusion. A determinable length,
breadth or height is a measurable dimension, and such dimensions
are defined operationally by specifying the standard and procedure.
There is no problem, apart from the technical, about measuring things.
The length, breadth or height of any familiar thing may be measured
by some invariant standard within certain limits of accuracy, whether
this is done by stretching a tape measure along it, or indirectly by
theodolite and triangulation, or by some other means. Shape may
also be specified geometrically by the additional measurement of angles
and curves. And so by other means for volume, weight, density,

D   35

specific gravity. This is what quantitative determination means. It is nonsense to say that a quantity is determinate when it cannot in principle be determined, and that, as I shall show, is precisely what is alleged when appearances of things are held to be of determinate size. When something is measured in the standard way, the result in feet and inches or in metres and centimetres is said to be *the* length or breadth or height. Whether the thing is fifty miles away or close at hand, no matter how anyone sees it or how it looks, these are its measurements which may be verified. That is what objective measurement, quantitative determination, means. (It can of course be vastly more complicated and indirect than my simple examples suggest, but my point is not affected.)

Measurement is taken so much for granted, that people often talk happily about real and apparent size without realising that they are talking about what, in a peculiar sense, are incommensurables ; the sense being that one of them is not mensurable. The size of a thing as seen is always an apparent size. To see the real size of something is to estimate how big it actually is from the look of it, from the apparent size, taking account of the distance and comparison with other things of known size. The notion of real or actual or objective size is incomprehensible without reference to measurement. The estimation of height and distance depends on practice and experience, and no doubt, since some people are hopeless at it, on some kind of flair. With practice, on familiar territory, it becomes prompt and rapid; a look is enough. One can then say, loosely, that one sees the real size. Similarly the practised eye can see the weight of a bullock. But no one, so far as I know, speaks of the real and apparent weights of a bullock: it would make just as good sense, and would indeed form an exact parallel to the way in which the expressions " real size " and " apparent size " are commonly used. A standard of measurement can be very rough, one's own height, for example. If one is of average height and one finds a man when close at hand " much smaller than he looked" it is not difficult to see what standard one is using from long habit.

Since things look bigger when they are nearer and smaller when they are further away, in a certain sense – perspectively – it is sometimes supposed that the actual height of the appearance to an observer at any point is determinate, that is that it can be determined by measurement. But this is not so. If one holds a ruler at arm's length, closes one eye, and " measures " a distant tree against the ruler, the tree already looks different, i.e. the appearance has already changed. Even so, one measures neither the height of the tree nor the height of the appearance of the tree. One could roughly measure the tree in this way if one knew the distance from the eye to the ruler and from the ruler to the tree. Very roughly! But merely by holding up the ruler and looking at what the tree " measures " against it, one has not measured anything. Has one not measured the height of the appearance of the tree to someone standing where one is standing? Again no. For if one holds the ruler at half arm's length, the tree measures less on the ruler than it does at full arm's length. And if one thinks to specify that the ruler must be held at full arm's length, what one is doing is treating the tree as if it were a picture of a tree on which the ruler is laid. But the tree is not at arm's length, nor is the appearance of the tree. If the tree or the appearance of it were a picture and the ruler laid on it, the distance from it of the eye would make no difference to the measurement. The appearance is not a picture, but even to appear to measure it, one must treat it as if it were a picture at a specified distance from the eye. This distance is entirely arbitrary. This kind of " measurement " is indeed used to get the proportions right for a drawing. But one is not measuring the appearances. One would be if they were pictures at a certain distance from the eye. But they are not. One can measure the two lines drawn on the blackboard to produce the Müller-Lyer illusion: they are found to be equal. One cannot measure the apparent inequality and say how much longer one appears than the other. Similarly, one cannot measure the angle of apparent convergence of the lines in the Zöllner illusion, nor how much bigger the moon appears at the horizon than at the zenith.

The assumption that the size and shape of appearances are determinate or determinable makes some discussions of the constancies of size and shape unintelligible. It is sometimes supposed that the relative sizes of things as we see them could be compared with or measured against their relative sizes as these are projected on the retina or on a photographic plate where we are standing. This of course is a fallacy:

they cannot be compared for there is nothing to compare. What we see as we see it, is not another picture or an image like the one on the retina, but simply the thing itself as we see it. That is all an appearance is. All sizes of things as we see them are apparent sizes.

An appearance, like a mental image, is nowhere. It is not an object, and not, as Kant would say, determinable as an object. The house I look at over there through the window is so determinable – its dimensions, the materials and their properties. But not the appearance of the house. The two sides of the house and the roof I can see from here are not the appearance: they are the parts of the house that are visible from here. They are determinable as objects. To determine the appearance one would have to find it, and where is it? Not where the house is, not where the eye is, not on the retina, and nowhere in between. But there is an appearance? Only in a sense analogous to that in which there are mental images. The appearance of the house is simply my seeing the house, how I see the house, the house as I see it, how the house looks to me, the look of the house. There is an appearance in the same sense as there is a look. But all that comes between the house and me is the ground and the other things on it – two treees, a wall, a shed and some grass, possibly a haze.

But isn't the appearance, it may be asked, smaller from here than if you were standing on the grass? Translated, this question runs: Doesn't the house look smaller from here than it would if you were standing on the grass? There are two answers to this. (1) Yes, that's because I'm further away from it than if I were standing on the grass. (2) No, it looks the same size but further away than if I were standing on the grass. To give one answer and think of the other is to find it no less true.

It is obviously true that things look smaller the further away they are – at the limit they can be mere specks on the horizon. It is no less true that, for example, the Pan Am building in New York can still look enormous, and indeed peculiarly enormous, at a distance of six or seven miles. But things look the way they look, the way we see them. " The way they look to us " and " the way we see them " are correlative and interchangeable expressions. The things as we see them, the way we see them, is the way they look to us. That is what appearances are, the looks of things. An appearance cannot have a determinate size or shape, because it is not a thing. Nor is it anywhere, nor in two dimensions, nor in three. One may say indifferently that one sees or observes the thing, or the look or appearance of the thing, but the look or appearance of the thing is merely the way the thing looks as one sees it. Looks are not determinable as objects, for they are not objects.

The view that " our sight informs us not of distance or outness (so to speak) immediately and without a certain reasoning and experience, as is acknowledg'd by the most rational philosophers " leads almost infallibly to the illusion of real appearances. The appearance thus hypostatised is easily assimilable to the hypostatised mental image, which is indeed at no distance whatsoever, since it is not in space at all, but which is regarded as a sort of picture, and of course pictures are flat. Hume constantly assumes that visual perception was " originally " in the flat, not in depth, but never explains how depth is derived from breadth and height, nor how breadth and height could be perceived at no distance at all. The problem is not to know what it is to see in depth – that is the way we do see – but what it would be like not to. What could " seeing two-dimensionally " possibly mean? How could we see in two if we didn't see in three? By this, I do not mean how we could see things or patches side by side or one above the other if we did not see one before or behind the other, but how we could see them side by side if we were in the same flat plane as them. Where would the plane be?

Hume, perhaps because he realised the absurdity, never mentions babies in this connection, though it is very hard to imagine what two-dimensional seeing could refer to except the way babies might naïvely be supposed to see. The power and ability to see, to fixate, develop in the first few months after birth. At what point an infant can reasonably be said to be seeing things is not very easy to determine. Sight continues normally to develop thereafter. But it is entirely meaningless to say that an infant sees two-dimensionally, ever.

Though the distinction is simple, the confusion is often made between seeing in depth and judging distance according to some measure or even saying which of two distances is the longer. Judging distances is very tricky. Seeing in depth is not. To see is to see in depth. To see anything is to look at it, fix it, attend to it, make it the figure of the Gestalt. To do this, it has to be at a distance. If it is too close, it cannot be seen – you must draw your head back to get a sight of it. To see something is to see what it is or to try to make out what it is. When something moves in the margin of vision, what we see is movement; to see what it is, we must look and fix it. One isn't seeing anything properly when one is day-dreaming with the eyes open – except intermittently – for to see anything is to look at it, attend to it, whether it is a broad landscape or some particular feature of it. Whatever is seen is seen at some distance.

The distance to the house I see is determinable just like the height of the house. Just as the dimensions of the house may be measured, so may the ground between the house and me. But the look of the distance cannot be measured any more than the look of the house. What I see is of course the ground, the two trees, the wall, the shed, ranged between the house and me, and covering a certain distance: let me call that ' the distance ' for short. For the house to look as it does, the distance must look as it does. To see the house as we see it, we must see the distance as we see it, and to see the distance as we see it, we must see the house as we see it. One does not see the house *and* the distance but the house at a distance or the distance to the house. The look of the house and of the distance, that is to say, are parts of a whole, of a configuration, or ensemble or Gestalt. Their relations are internal, not external: they mutually imply each other. That is why one can give two answers to the question: Does the house look smaller from here than if you were standing on the grass? When one says " yes ", one is attending rather to the look of the house. When one says " no ", one is attending rather to the look of the distance. There is of course no contradiction, for the look of the house or the distance, the appearances, are simply the way we see the house at a distance or the distance to the house.

In estimating what the distance is, there is no doubt at all about the importance of " reasoning and experience ". Open-air people can judge distances well in their own territories, whether in temporal (" time to walk ") or spatial terms, but not in other territories where the atmosphere is clearer or hazier, the trees more or less numerous, and so on. What one learns is what things look like when they are, say, a mile away under various conditions in this territory. An actual distance as measured cannot be compared with an apparent distance but only with what you judge the distance to be. The look of the distance, the distance as you see it, cannot be compared with *anything* but only with another look, any more than the height of the house as you see it can be compared with the measured height of the house. Some people achieve remarkable accuracy in estimating heights, lengths and distances. It is as if they could see the mileage. But unless one has occasion to make such estimates for one purpose or another, one just does not do it. One sees things in reach or near or further or far away. But beyond the reach of the arm it is not easy without deliberate practice to guess how far. One has to calculate how far it is even to the wall of the room. But one sees where the wall is and the floor from here to the wall. One can only measure the distance, not the distance as we see it, not the appearance of the distance, not the look of the floor from here to the wall, but only the floor itself.

If I seem to have laboured the point that to see is to see in depth, my excuse must be that it is frequently forgotten. It is rarely denied; people just forget it or fail to realise what it means. I have mentioned one sort of absurdity which crops up in discussion of the constancies: the suggestion that real and apparent sizes can be compared. Another example is the suggestion that the depth of the circular rim of a bowl as drawn by a normal person represents a compromise between the circularity which he knows it to have and the retinal projection. This kind of view really amounts to the old judgmental, intellectualist theory of perception, possibly transferred to the " unconscious " and therefore beyond the reach of argument. What the normal person draws is an attempt to represent the bowl as he sees it, the way it looks. Essentially the same point crops up in discussions of how the words " circle " and " square " come to be applied to so many different " apparent " shapes, i.e. skew projections of circles and squares. To understand this " problem " at all one has to assume that these different shapes are all in the flat. If that were so it would be quite impossible to imagine how the different shapes could ever be recognised as circular or square. But these words are simply not applied to skew projections of circles and squares. They are applied to things seen in depth. I could not see the penny lying flat on the window-sill six feet away if I saw it end-on. There is no skew projection of the penny as we see it, nor was there ever. What we see is a penny at an angle.

To see things in depth is to see them from where one is and therefore as having another side which is out of sight. It is not necessary, and it is indeed implausible, to suppose that children who draw a face in profile with both eyes staring straight out are doing anything but trying to represent the other side as well. The face is seen as having another side with another eye corresponding to this one. The representation of what is visible in more or less " photographic " proportions has to be learned somewhat laboriously. But if some theories of perception had any foundation this is what one would expect children to do naturally.

The standard blackboard illusions are appearances of a kind which we normally never consider illusory, partly because we do not go around measuring the sizes of things we see and comparing one size with another. The Müller-Lyer illusion admirably illustrates a commonplace: that measurably equal lengths or areas on one surface can look very different. This fact is constantly exploited in architecture. To cite a very simple example, the wall of a building may be given height by putting tall narrow windows in the ground floor and somewhat shorter ones above. Though the wall is square, it will look taller than it is wide. If the apparent inequality of the lines in the Müller-Lyer is to be called illusory – and in a sense it is illusory – it is important to remember that a vast proportion of our perceptual experience is also illusory by the same token. The reason for doubting whether one ought to call it illusory is that it is normally quite reliable and lets us down mainly where measurement is required, e.g. when we buy a pair of curtains that *look* the right size for our window. Two measurably equal rooms can look quite different in size according to the décor. The same room can look cramped or spacious. The decorator learns what makes rooms look bigger, taller, or wider; the dressmaker learns what slims fat women, narrows broad shoulders, etc. One of the commonest illusions is that the eyes are in the upper half of the head. Another is that the legs are very much longer than the arms.

Hypostatised appearances and images and the illusion of immanence all belong to the same kind of doctrine, in which what we call "things" have somehow to be constructed out of these hypostases regarded as data. In my view nothing can be regarded as a datum, a pure datum, or rather only our ongoing, actual perceptual experience. All one can do is to analyse that. On this view, the appearance of a thing is the look of it, the way it looks to me, the way I see it. Without the seeing and the seen, me and it, there could be no appearance. This not only seems tautological; it is. To see is to see something from somewhere; to see it as one sees it is to see it as it looks. One cannot see anything except as it looks. This is not to deny, but to affirm and insist, that it looks, or may look, different when one has learned more about it, which mostly consists in looking and examining. But to regard the look or the appearance as an entity is to make a false hypostasis. The appearance is nowhere. Nor is the image anywhere.

Whether one is seeing or imagining, one is where one is bodily. In seeing, the object is present; it is it one sees and one sees it where it is from where one is oneself. But in imagining, it is not bodily present to one's own body, one's own eyes. One images it as one saw it, though it is not present to be looked at, to be explored and examined. One imagines it the way it looked, the configuration, the situation, the physiognomy. In remembering a pretty girl, one may have forgotten – if one ever noticed – the colour of the eyes, the length of the nose, how far the hair came down the neck; one cannot look, for there is nothing to look at. But one remembers the expression, the smile, the charm, the twinkle in the eye, the walk – the look, the appearance.

CHAPTER SIX

THINGS AND APPEARANCES

THE objective characteristics of anything are the determinable, verifiable characteristics, to be determined by standard procedures under standard conditions, which are never completely specified. But is a thing not reducible to all its appearances – all the looks of the thing? No: neither to one of the appearances, nor to all of them, whatever " all " might mean. But it is apprehended or constituted as one thing through the appearances: the diverse and changing appearances.

Let us take for example a house. There is no look, no appearance apart from the way I see the house, the way it looks to me. As I walk round it, the look changes, but the house is like the ground under my feet: it stays where it is and does not change position. It is because it stays where it is that the appearance changes as I move. If the front did not " close up " as the side comes into view and "broadens out", I would not be moving bodily, or seeing in depth. I never cease to see what I see there in depth as a house, which stays still while I move. If the appearance were not changing as I move, the house would not be staying where it is. It looks different from different places, but it is by virtue of looking different that it stays the same. I do not just see an oblong shape from straight in front, and a narrowing quadrilateral shape with two parallel and two converging boundaries when I move to one side. I see an oblong shape head-on and an oblong shape at an angle, staying where it is as I move to one side.

If the oblong were not foreshortened when looked at from one side it would have ceased to be an oblong, or it would have moved with me. If the appearance, the look of the house, had not changed, the house would have moved, or I would not have moved. One's own movement over the ground as well as by turning the head and body and eyes is an essential part of perceptual experience. Movement is in depth and what one sees is in depth in the same space. Things would not be seen in depth if they did not look different from different places.

Theories which reduce things to their appearances usually treat the appearances as flat projections on photographic plates, in spite of the fact that a house or a tree, for example, never looks flat except when seen in silhouette or through a fog, and even then is seen at some distance. It is never explained how a third dimension can be derived from two. To treat appearances as appearances in depth, on the other hand, is already to treat them as appearances of things having another side as well as the visible one.

The first condition of determination is abstraction, conceptualisation. It is always in some respect that a thing is determined: length, weight, volume, mass, melting point, boiling point, acidity. Determination need not be quantitative, but it is always, as it were, dimensional: the use of litmus to determine acidity is an example. But in the last resort a determinable characteristic is measurable directly or indirectly. It is a dimension, defined operationally. The primary qualities were such dimensions, and the distinction between the primary and the secondary qualities was at bottom between those which had been found reducible to measure and those which had not.

But determination always depends in the last resort on direct observation. To measure the length of a wall in the ordinary way the tape must be held against one end of the wall and seen to be against it, or held parallel to it and seen to be parallel to it. The only means of deciding whether any measurement is correct is by checking and re-checking, directly or indirectly. But what is measured is not the look of the measure and the wall, but the wall by the measure.

In giving an account of perceptual experience, chiefly in terms of seeing, my purpose so far has been partly to show that the notion of raw data occurring to a disembodied consciousness (or in later versions just occurring and associating) is unintelligible in relation to actual experience and at best wildly hypothetical as regards infantile experience. To be a body, an embodied self, is to be in space in a world of things. From the standpoint of the older physiology and, following it, the older psychology, sense experience was essentially reducible to the action of a physically determinate environment on the several specialised senses. The resulting data had no intrinsic connection and had by regular concomitance to become associated. The theory has long since lost its supposed physiological basis: the effect of any stimulus is complex and has to be understood in terms ultimately of the whole organism. But quite apart from that, actual sense experience could not be deduced from any physiological theory. This experience is of a world which is accessible to sight and touch. A thing we see is at a distance; we can move towards it and touch it. We do not have data to be correlated, associated, and brought together into things. The same thing is accessible to sight and touch. The tangible is seen and the visible is touched.

Strict data doctrines cannot say anything about actual perceptual experience, about the experience of seeing, touching, hearing, moving about. Nor can they, for example, make the important distinction between touching and being touched, or between merely having one's eyes open and actually looking at things, or between the figure and ground of a Gestalt. They cannot officially and explicitly admit that perception is indissolubly connected with embodiment and movement, with being in the world, in the midst of things, being " here " as a body and seeing things " there ". Data cannot be seen and touched, for to see is to see with one's eyes, and to touch is to touch with some part of one's body. These facts are smuggled in surreptitiously by classifying data as visual, tactual and kinaesthetic, as if visuality, tactuality and kinaestheticity were properties of the data. (Consciousness or awareness, if it is admitted, is essentially disembodied and passively receptive.) I say " surreptitiously " for, while it could not be admitted that a datum was visible without admitting that it could be seen, and therefore inviting the question " where ?", it is evidently supposed that it can be plausibly said to be visual without being ever actually seen or see-able.

As I have already remarked, the mind and its activities and propensities, which figure prominently throughout the *Treatise*, do not form part of the " system " though the system could hardly be described without reference to them. Again, whenever Hume appeals to the reader's experience as he frequently does, his appeal is to reflexion, but he has no explicit doctrine of reflexion. What must be taken to be his most considered account of belief as it is given in the Appendix (*Treatise*, pp. 628-9) identifies belief with the manner of conceiving an idea, and is of course a reflexive description. Similarly that " the imagination has the command over all its ideas " could only be known reflexively. The same point could be made of other passages throughout the *Treatise*. For any description of experience of the world, of subjective experience, as distinct from the objective determination of things, is reflexive. Everyone, every day, offers reflexive descriptions. " I see " is reflexive, and this is not simply a matter of the pronoun: my evidence that anyone else sees depends in the last resort on my seeing and this can only be known reflexively by actually seeing. So commonplace and indispensable is reflexion that it is commonly denied, as for instance by Ryle, who employs it constantly in *The Concept of Mind*.

Hume, as I say, has no explicit doctrine of reflexion but some of the most perplexing things about his doctrine have, I think, to be attributed to his failure to recognise it. The most important of these is the identification of the consciousness of the object and the object of consciousness in the " perception ", the hypostatised appearance and mental image, in which seeing and imagining coalesce with the object seen or imagined. But for Hume, the hypostatised impression or idea is itself an object of consciousness. The sense in which it may be so regarded is that in which we may be reflexively aware of seeing or imagining something. To be aware of a mental image as such is simply to be reflexively aware of imaging something.

To Hume's hypostasis of the mental image and the appearance may be traced that version of his doctrine of belief which states that it is the liveliness of an idea. This distortion of the language reflects Hume's identification of the imagining and what is imagined. Whereas " belief " would in ordinary language be ascribed to the subject or consciousness, it is here apparently ascribed to the object or rather identified with the liveliness of the object – the idea. But the perceptions are themselves also regarded as objects, and his subsequent account of belief is that the mind is enlivened by impressions and itself enlivens the attendant ideas.

47

But a further complication is that belief tends to be identified with an " impression of reflexion ", that is to say, with a feeling or passion or sentiment. Hume for obvious reasons never refers to these as objects, but he does regard them frequently as identifiable and distinctive events or occurrences, which may be, as it were, observed. Each passion is specifically different from the others and is recognisable as such. What I have said of the impression of sensation, that it is at once consciousness and object, is also true of the impression of reflexion.

CHAPTER SEVEN

THE PHYSIOLOGY OF
THE PASSIONS

In Hume's theory of knowledge as it is presented in the third and fourth parts of Book I, the independently existing world, the world of nature, consists of systematically related fictions of the imagination, objects of belief, and the occurrence of the impressions and ideas cannot therefore be ascribed to natural causes. But in the first two sections of Book I, and especially in Book II, the physiological theory on which the doctrine of impressions and ideas was based emerges clearly, and this theory of course presupposes a physical world.

To illustrate, here is a quaint example from Book I, where Hume is accounting for the mistakes arising from the relations of contiguity and resemblance among ideas:

'Twou'd have been easy to have made an imaginary dissection of the brain, and have shewn, why upon our conception of any idea, the animal spirits run into all the contiguous traces, and rouze up the other ideas, that are related to it. But tho' I have neglected any advantage, which I might have drawn from this topic in explaining the relations of ideas, I am afraid I must here have recourse to it, in order to account for the mistakes that arise from these relations. I shall therefore observe, that as the mind is endow'd with a power of exciting any idea it pleases; whenever it dispatches the spirits into that region of the brain, in which the idea is plac'd; these spirits always excite the idea, when they run precisely into the proper traces, and rummage that cell, which belongs to the idea. But as their motion is seldom direct, and naturally turns a little to the one side or the other; for this reason the animal spirits, falling into the contiguous traces, present other

49

related ideas in lieu of that, which the mind desir'd at first to survey. This change we are not always sensible of; but continuing still the same train of thought, make use of the related idea, which is presented to us and employ it in our reasoning, as if it were the same with what we demanded. This is the cause of many mistakes and sophisms in philosophy; as will naturally be imagin'd, and as it wou'd be easy to shew, if there was occasion.

(*Treatise*, pp. 60-1)

The same physiological theory underlies Hume's causal theory of the passions; the impressions of sensation are physically caused and themselves cause the impressions of reflexion:

Original impressions or impressions of sensation are such as without any antecedent perception arise in the soul, from the constitution of the body, from the animal spirits, or from the application of objects to the external organs. Secondary, or reflective impressions are such as proceed from some of these original ones, either immediately or by the interposition of its idea. Of the first kind are all the impressions of the senses, and all bodily pains and pleasures: Of the second are the passions, and other emotions resembling them.

'Tis certain, that the mind, in its perceptions, must begin somewhere; and that since the impressions precede their correspondent ideas, there must be some impressions, which without any introduction make their appearance in the soul. As these depend upon natural and physical causes, the examination of them wou'd lead me too far from my present subject, into the sciences of anatomy and natural philosophy. For this reason I shall here confine myself to those other impressions, which I have call'd secondary and reflective, as arising either from the original impressions, or from their ideas. Bodily pains and pleasures are the source of many passions, both when felt and consider'd by the mind; but arise originally in the soul, or in the body, whichever you please to call it, without any preceding thought or perception.

(*Treatise*, pp. 275-6)

Bodily pains and pleasures are both in the soul and in the body. From the physiological standpoint which underlies his doctrine the same can be said of all impressions whatsoever. For "every impression, external and internal, passions, affections, sensations, pains and pleasures, are originally on the same footing; and that whatever other differences we may observe among them, they appear, all of them, in their true colours, as impressions or perceptions." (*Treatise*, p. 190) Though he generally reserves the expression "impressions of sensation" for the primary impressions, the secondary impressions are in effect sensations too. Hume sometimes distinguishes between the emotions and the passions, or between the sensations of the passions and the passions, whose character is determined by "the general bent or tendency" (*Treatise*, p. 385), and it is evident that what he means by the passion of pride, for example, is the circumstances of its occurrence as well as the occurrence itself. But all the impressions are felt, and how should they be felt but bodily? But if so, how are what we call "bodily pains and pleasures" distinguished from other sensations?

Hume never expounds the physiological theory on which he relies, but it seems to be essentially similar to the one which Descartes presents in *Les Passions de l'Âme*. The passions are caused by the movement of the animal spirits. Descartes uses the word "passion" in a wider and a narrower sense. In the wider sense, passion is opposed to action, and some ideas, which for Hume are copies of impressions, and which are called by Descartes "imaginations", are strictly speaking passions. But Descartes on the whole takes passions in exactly the same sense as Hume. They are "perceptions, or sentiments, or emotions of the soul, which are related especially to it, and which are caused, and sustained, and fortified by some movement of the spirits" (*Passions*, Art. 27). Sentiments are sensations, as Descartes makes clear in Art. 28: "One may also name them sentiments, because they are received in the soul in the same fashion as the objects of the external senses and are known by it in the same way." As he goes on to explain in Art. 29, other "sentiments" we relate to external objects such as odours, sounds and colours, and others to our own body, such as hunger, thirst and pain. But since "the soul is united to all the parts of the body conjointly", a sentiment is evidently in both soul and

E

body, or, as Hume says, " in the soul, or in the body, whichever you please to call it ".

Thus, from the physiological standpoint, Hume's view is near enough to Descartes'. Perhaps this is to say no more than that physiological doctrines from the time of Descartes to that of Hume have a resemblance. But it is likely enough that Hume had read Descartes' treatise, and that he regarded all sensations as being in a sense in the body, though only some—the bodily pains and pleasures—were referred to the body. (In his *other* doctrine, I repeat, the body is, like any other body, a fiction of the imagination, and the imagination is as it were a pure disembodied consciousness.)

A further passage which casts some light on the matter occurs in the *Treatise*, Book II, part 2, Section viii, 'Of malice and envy'. It is of interest from several points of view. In it, Hume discusses the effect of comparison, or contrast, in sense perception. He begins by remarking that men " always judge more of objects by comparison than from their intrinsic worth and value ". It might seem difficult to say what in his terms this last phrase " intrinsic worth and value " could strictly mean. This tendency to judge of things by comparison, he says, " is an *original* quality of the soul, and similar to what we have every day experience of in our bodies. . . . Any gentle pain, that follows a violent one, seems as nothing . . . a violent pain, succeeding a gentle one, is doubly grievous and uneasy."

The next paragraph is worth quoting as a whole:

This no one can doubt of with regard to our passions and sensations. But there may arise some difficulty with regard to our ideas and objects. When an object augments or diminishes to the eye or imagination from a comparison with others, the image and idea of the object are still the same, and are equally extended in the *retina*, and in the brain or organ of perception. The eyes refract the rays of light, and the optic nerves convey the images to the brain in the very same manner, whether a great or small object has preceded; nor does even the imagination alter the dimensions of its object on account of a comparison with others. The question then is, how from the same impression and the same idea we can form such different judgments concerning the same object, and at one time admire its bulk, and at another despise its littleness. This variation in our judgments must certainly proceed from a variation in some perception; but as the variation lies not in the immediate impression or idea of the object, it must lie in some other impression, that accompanies it.

It will be remembered that when Hume insists that our sight informs us not of outness, he insists that "properly speaking, 'tis not our body we perceive, when we regard our limbs and members, but certain impressions, which enter by the senses; so that the ascribing a real and corporeal existence to these impressions and to their objects, is an act of the mind as difficult to explain as that which we examine at present". But the only evidence for believing that our sight informs us not of outness is of the kind cited in the above passage – " the image and idea of the object are still the same, and are equally extended in the *retina*, and in the brain and organ of perception ".

There is a further curious point about this passage. Hume is saying that an impression can *look* bigger or smaller by contrast, though an impression strictly is as it appears, and is of determinate size. This paradox is a natural error resulting from the illusion of real appearances. The hypostatised appearance is treated as if it were a thing, and like a thing it can look bigger or smaller.

Hume's explanation is that the emotion is confused with the object: " ... no object is presented to the senses, nor image form'd in the fancy, but what is accompany'd with some emotion or movement of the spirits proportioned to it; and however custom may make us insensible of this sensation, and cause us to confound it with the object or idea, 'twill be easy, by careful and exact experiments, to separate and distinguish them ". Not content with this more or less plausible view, Hume is then carried away and proceeds to suggest that " every part of extension, and every unite of number [i.e. the "real" unit or *minimum sensibile*] has a separate emotion attending it . . . and though that emotion be not always agreeable, yet by its conjunction with others, and by its agitating the spirits to a just pitch, it contributes to the production of the admiration, which is always agreeable ". A great object is attended with a great emotion, a small object with a small. When a great succeeds a small, it " rises beyond its ordinary proportion " and " we naturally imagine that the object has likewise increased. . . . Those, who are acquainted with the metaphysical part of optics, and know how we transfer the judgments and conclusions of the understanding to the senses, will easily conceive this whole operation." (*Treatise*, pp 373–5)

My reason for dealing at some length with what many might consider the worst part of Hume's doctrine is that much of the better part rests upon it. Hume makes no deliberate distinction between the body as an object and the body as subject, sometimes treating it as the one and sometimes as the other without realising that there is any ambiguity. The confusion of perceptual and bodily experience with physiological and physical fact and theory is as common now as it was then. My essential contention is that one cannot make sense of either unless they are distinguished.

Hume, I believe, is right in regarding the passions as bodily, and right in thinking that emotion or affect is never absent from perception, in spite of the fantastic physical account which he attempts to give of this. His doctrine of the passions if of course mainly concerned with the more complexly conditioned social passions and sentiments: it constitutes the prolegomena to his theory of morals, with which I shall not be dealing. The point I am concerned with, however, is fundamental in his whole doctrine of the passions and of morals. For Hume, percepts *cause* affects; it follows from this that, among other things, all the passions, including the moral sentiments, are mechanically caused and likewise the moral judgments which express them.

But the foundations of the whole structure lie in physiology, where the term " impression " originates. Hume, as I have said, identifies the " impression " with what would ordinarily be called the appearance or look of something, and makes of this an entity and causal agent. Hume believes that the passion is caused by the external impression and is then projected back on to it, as it were, in the form of a value which may be predicated of it. There is no evidence for this in perceptual experience. As I shall argue, we see what we see as we see it, values and all. The only evidence Hume has for his view is of the kind which I have tried to illustrate above – evidence drawn from physiological and physical theory. At best, this would be an account, not of experience, but of its causes, how it comes to be as it is. But even as such it will not do, for no evidence of the looks or appearances of things is to be found in physical or physiological theory, but only in perceptual experience.

As I shall show, in the illusion of real appearances the colour, size and shape are held to be real because they are believed to be determinate. As I have argued, and shall argue further, not even the size and shape are determinate in the sense demanded by the theory. They are of equal status so far as this is concerned with the values. The physiological theory required that the values be left out of the external impression – the real appearance – hence in Hume's doctrine the impression or object derives whatever quality it may have apart from size, shape and colour from the emotions or passions it causes. The impression or real appearance in itself has size, shape and colour, but not pleasantness or unpleasantness, menace or invitation, warmth of colour, grandeur, grace or splendour. As the real appearance is an illusion, this theory of projection, whereby it appears to have some qualities which it does not really have, is doubly so.

CHAPTER EIGHT

THE DOMAIN OF VALUE

I<small>F</small> appearances are the way things look, the way we see them, qualities and values belong to the appearance. What one sees is the things, but one sees them only as one sees them – from a place, at a distance, looking big or massive or threatening or inviting or beautiful or ugly. One is not looking at the appearances – they are not there to be looked at – but at the things, which appear in a certain way and have a certain look; they are in certain surroundings, part of a certain configuration. That is the way we see them, the way they look, and that is the appearance, the look, and the expression they have.

But, it may be said, we do not literally see the splendour, grace, etc., of Salisbury Cathedral. No, I reply, in a sense you do not see the appearance at all; you see the cathedral. But that is the way you see it – clothed in the splendour of sunshine, just as you see it looking slender and graceful. But, it may be said, to say something is splendid, or graceful, or beautiful, is to make a value judgment. Yes, I say, whatever you see as you see it may be expressed in a statement or judgment – bigness, smallness, distance, dullness, hugeness, repulsiveness. But surely, it may be said, to say something is *big* is not to make a value judgment. To this I cannot say yes or no, but must say: isn't it?

A man who is six foot five is big and a man who is four foot ten is small: the former is much above the normal height, and the latter much below it, according to their measured heights. Again, you may say St Peter's is very big and St Paul's not very big, if you happen to know that St Peter's is three times the size of St Paul's – or whatever the measured proportion is. But the hugeness of St Peter's as you look at it across the square is not a matter of comparative measurements. Nor is the hugeness of St Paul's as you turn a corner into a narrow street and see it looming up and perhaps tilt your head back to see the top of the dome.

But, it may be said, you judge that it is huge because you have to tilt your head back, and the other buildings are small in comparison. Yes, I reply, but this account is somewhat misleading. I do not compare what I see with the size of the other buildings and the width of the street and the cars and people in it, and then, taking into account the fact that I have had to tilt my head, judge (i.e. conclude): this building must be huge. I am in a situation, a configuration which includes the street, the buildings and St Paul's, and I am *in* it, a part of it, neck, eyes, head and all. If I weren't, then of course St Paul's would not look huge. But I am, and it does: it looms up of a sudden and I see it as I see it – huge. If I then say "it's huge" or merely "big", what sort of judgment is this? It is certainly not an objective judgment of fact.

Size, proportion and scale in this context are matters of the look of things. A building would look different in another setting, and that includes looking bigger or smaller. It might make one scene and ruin another; dominate, dwarf and bully its neighbours or take a seemly part in the ensemble. Size in this context is a matter of the way the building looks or the way we see it, and we don't all see it the same way. "Huge", "enormous", "tiny", "giant", "dwarf", all belong fairly obviously to this kind of talk. So, much of the time, do "big" and "small". The same of course goes for heaviness and lightness of weight or softness and loudness of sound; these expressions do not primarily refer to any sort of measurement at all: a thing feels heavy in a sense analogous to that in which it looks big.

It is because of their secondary meaning in connection with measurement and comparison of measured quantities and sizes, that one might suppose otherwise in the case of "big" and "small". This secondary use may be called their conventional use.[1] Size, scale and proportion in the primary sense are inseparable. The size of a building is a

---

[1] There is some sort of parallel, though I would not care to press it too far, with the use of ' good ' to express approval or commendation and its conventional use according to set standards and criteria. See R. M. Hare, *The Language of Morals*, chap. 7 (London: O.U.P., 1952) on description and evaluation.

function of its setting, its relation to the other buildings and the land-scape or townscape. The only other meaning of size is measured size. Size in the primary sense is what is called a value in architecture and the visual arts, and it is not easy to make the distinction between a value in this sense and a quality. In the case of colour, one might think to distinguish between the quality – red, say – and the value in the picture – fieriness, say. But this is quite arbitrary. At any rate, size is a value or a quality in the same sense as colour or shape: a dis-tinguishable aspect which is not, however, separable from the others but is an organic part of the whole appearance, the way the thing looks, the way we see it.

To alter the size of one building is to change the proportions of other buildings to it and sometimes to each other, to make them look bigger or smaller. To change the colour is also often to change the size. But what one sees, as one sees it, is not usually analysed in this way: when one sees an enormous building, though this is very much a matter of setting, proportion and scale, the building is the figure and the rest the ground, and the enormity is apprehended as a quality of the building. Hence we may be surprised by a change in its appear-ance, when so far as we can discover it has remained objectively un-changed: the demolition of a nearby building or the felling of trees can do this.

It is difficult to distinguish aesthetic values from values in the above sense, for the analysis of the aesthetic value of a building, a sculpture, a park or a painting, for example, is in terms of such values as these, which are integral parts of the whole. Nor is it easy to make the dis-tinction between a *mere* description of the way a thing looks and an aesthetic judgment. To say a building is big is not, except in a special context, to make an aesthetic judgment. But to say it is soaring or towering or massive is to verge upon it; to say it is slender is almost to say it is graceful, and this would commonly be regarded as an aesthetic judgment.

If anyone wants to insist with Hume, for example, that utility or fitness for purpose is the major part of the beauty of things and forms the basis of aesthetic judgment, I would certainly not dissent. We are doers as well as perceivers and it is as doers that we often perceive.

Nor do we all see things the same way – they do not look the same to all of us or to any of us all the time. The " conquest of nature " had not proceeded far enough before the nineteenth century for men to see the Alps as anything but a horrid waste of snow, ice and rocks where little could be grown, though perhaps a useful barrier against the depredations of other men. In the industrial age the Alps were seen with new eyes : they looked different, and part of the attraction, I would surmise, was that there was no utility or fitness for any sort of serious purpose about them. A matter of contrast, or comparison, as Hume would say, of their pure, unsullied, useless white and the dark, Satanic, very useful mills. I make this short foray into socio-aesthetic history in order to insist that however we come to see things as we do, we do see things as we do, and this is the way they look. Nor can we ever see them except as they look.

Let us now turn to the expressions of things. Things as we see them can have an expression or physiognomy. Sometimes one wants to make some sort of distinction between the expression and the look and sometimes not. Let me say evasively that it is when a look expresses something that I want to call it an expression. The most obvious case of expressions are those on people's faces. A face always has an expression; its expressions are, as it were, modulations of its characteristic look. Blankness and impassivity are of course expressions too. But no less obviously landscapes, buildings, streets, rooms, furniture and ships have expressions as we see them, or *can* have at least – it depends on the way you look at them – and for many of these the same words are used as for facial expressions: cold, warm, hostile, grim, friendly, welcoming, comfortable, complacent, proud, smug, uneasy, smiling, open, closed, secretive, confident, rakish, raffish and so on. The expressions again are modifications of the characteristic look. A landscape is seen as expressing moods. Animism and the pathetic fallacy are well-founded in perceptual experience, especially in childhood. Places are sympathetic or unsympathetic. One is at home or not at home in a new place, as one is, or not, with new people. If Mr Gradgrind were to say " Gibberish ! " that would be because he is concerned with facts, determinate, objectively verifiable facts about things, not with the looks and expressions of things.

But even Mr Gradgrind can only see things as he sees them, as they look. Looks and expressions are not things or facts.

Some philosophers want to deny these commonplaces, while admitting they are commonplaces. The grounds on which objections are raised to the kind of thing I have been saying are: (1) that the expressions of things are illusions; that things do not really have expressions; (2) that the expressions of things are the projections of our feelings; (3) that the smugness or grimness or other expression of a thing is not at any rate a perceptual phenomenon: what is perceived is shape, size and colour, not smugness or grimness or cheekiness.

To (1) I reply: as determinate objects, reduced to their properties and measurable dimensions, things have no expression. Neither do they have a look, an appearance. But we see them as we see them, from where we are, in a certain light, context and configuration, and as they look to us, with a certain expression.

To (2) I reply: a thing cannot look as it does look except to someone who is looking at it, for its look is the way it looks to someone, and the expression belongs to the look. The projection theory of which one form is to be found in Hume – " the propensity of the mind to spread itself upon external objects " – is not in itself an objection: it is a theory which attempts to account for the expressions of things, to say how they come to have or seem to have expressions. I shall offer some objections to this view later.

To (3) I reply: if we do not *see* the smugness or the grimness, or the grace or elegance, how is it that we think the thing looks smug or grim or graceful or elegant, and say it is smug, etc.? If the grace or grimness is not visible, how do we apprehend it? If it has an elegant shape, say, is the shape seen but not its elegance? But, it may be said, the shape is there objectively; it can be determined, described and measured. That is indeed so, I reply, but not the shape as you see it, the look of the shape, and as you see it it is elegant or otherwise.

The objection underlying (3) is generally founded on some doctrine of the sensationalist or datum type. To explain how a doctrine so implausible so far as our actual perceptual experience goes should have been widely believed, I think one must look at the question historically. Let us go back to Plato's discussion of sense-perception in the

Theaetetus. What is apt to surprise the modern reader is the puzzles about size and number at 154C. "When you compare six dice with four, we say that the six are more than the four or half as many again; while if you compare them with twelve, the six are fewer – only half as many – and one cannot say anything else." Theaetetus agrees and Socrates asks: "Can anything become larger or more otherwise than by being increased? What will you answer?" Theaetetus answers "no" to this question (154D).

Socrates continues (155A):

> Looking at the first of them, I suppose we shall assert that nothing can become greater or less, either in size or number, so long as it remains equal to itself. . . . And secondly, that a thing to which nothing is added and from which nothing is taken away is neither increased nor diminished, but always remains the same in amount. . . . And must we not say, thirdly, that a thing which was not at an earlier moment cannot be at a later moment without becoming and being in process of becoming? . . . Now these three admissions, I fancy, fight among themselves in our minds when we make those statements about the dice; or when we say that I, being of the height you see, without gaining or losing in size, may within a year be taller (as I am now) than a youth like you, and later on be shorter, not because I have lost anything in bulk, but because you have grown. For apparently I am later what I was not before, and yet have not become so; for without the process of becoming the result is impossible, and I could not be in process of becoming shorter without losing some of my bulk. Of such puzzles, Theaetetus says, "Sometimes I get quite dizzy with thinking of them."

> (F. M. Cornford, *Plato's Theory of Knowledge*, pp. 42–3)

But the problem for the modern reader is to know what Theaetetus's problem is. It arises from regarding size and number as qualities of things on the one hand and as relations between things on the other. As qualities they cannot change without the thing "becoming". As relations they can – only the other term must "become". As Cornford remarks, the difficulty "exists only for one who thinks of 'large' as a quality residing in the thing which is larger than something else, with ' small ' as the answering quality residing in the smaller thing ". When compared with something larger it will lose its quality " large " and gain the quality " small ". Cornford notes that in the *Phaedo* Plato regards tallness as an inherent property of the tall person. He adds that tallness was commonly ranked as a physical excellence with beauty, health and strength. It was a property on the same footing as hot or white, and not a relation between the taller person and the shorter (*Plato's Theory of Knowledge*, pp. 43–4).

It is natural to dismiss the problem, since obviously all size is relative. But so are all other properties: the colour of anything, for example, is relative to other colours. One blue is bluer than another blue (greenish-blue or purplish-blue), and one white whiter than another white; and of course contrast intensifies colour. Similarly heat and cold are relative. And these are regarded as properties of things in ordinary experience. But so in a way is size: a building is big of course by virtue of its surroundings, but we naturally ascribe this property to the building – the figure – and forget the ground.

It is only in terms of measurement, objective determination, that the problem disappears, for then we are no longer concerned with the mere look of things, the way we see them, and size and quantity become explicitly relative to a standard measure. Obviously nothing is " in itself " big or small. But just as obviously, some things are huge and some tiny as we see them; that is the way they look. The modern tendency, in thinking of size and quantity, is to forget the looks of things and to regard all bigness and smallness as matters of measure, of relation to a standard. Since the sixteenth century, objective determination has meant the reduction of quality to measurable quantity. The first candidate for such reduction long before then was size: length, breadth, height and volume. It is easily forgotten that size was, and is, a quality in the first place. The assumption is that all things are in themselves fully determinate – all qualities are determinable by reduction to measurable dimensions, even if this has not actually been accomplished.

The doctrine that the real is the rational in its most prevalent and indeed triumphant form has for its corollary that the rational is the measurable. But this is not the world as it is lived and experienced directly, the world of values where things have a physiognomy, a look, and look different – bigger or smaller – at different times and bear expressions: the world as we perceive it. Though everyone all the time lives and moves and has his being in this world, it was not much studied. Hume's account of it was tailored to what was scientifically "known" and as we have seen the "impression" is in origin a physiological concept. The procedure of physics required the exclusion from consideration of residual quality and value, or at best their relegation to the status of secondary effects of the physically real upon organic bodies. Direct experience, it was thought, could be causally explained in physical terms.

Of the impressions, it will be recalled, Hume says: "As these depend upon natural and physical causes, the examination of them would lead me too far from my present subject, into the sciences of anatomy and natural philosophy." (*Treatise*, p. 275).

He assumes the causal relation *could* be shown even if it never *had* been, and the impressions would be natural events causally connected with other events and processes. This is of course a natural assumption. For example, colours as we perceive them are associated with reflected light of different wavelengths. Hume's account of the senses, especially of the visual sense, takes the impressions of sense to be the effects of physical causes, and to be, like everything in nature, determinate in quantity. These are the data of consciousness and as they are really – fully determinate – so they appear.

But our perceptual experience is not of impressions, but of things at rest or in motion, changing or unchanging. Physical science starts with these things: these are what its laws are about – bodies, bits of stuff. If these were not constituted perceptually in the first place, there would be nothing to determine quantitatively in any dimension. Abstraction is abstraction from the concrete. The illusion on which Hume's and other similar theories of perception are based is that our perception of things may be accounted for in terms of physical laws, laws which are first of all about the things which we perceive – bodies, gross matter.

Taking for granted the physical and physiological processes dis-covered by observation and experiment, the theorist tries to complete the cycle or close the circle and account for experience. But the datum of experience is not a physical event. So it must be a mental event. The theory then merely succeeds in making the notion of physical bodies unintelligible; we first took these to be the things we see and went to work to reduce them to their quantitative dimensions. We finish by holding – if we make the matter explicit – that the bodies we have thus reduced are not those we suppose we see. Our seeing and what we see are then identified and the resultant entity is called a per-ception or mental event, physically caused. Hume is both the victim of this doctrine and the rebel against it, but even as the rebel his premises are those of the doctrine.

In his and similar later doctrines, the looks of things are hypostatised as perceptions or percepts, and things are held to be inferred entities, posits, postulates or objects of belief. But, as I have tried to show, things are constituted visibly through their appearances to an observer in depth perception, neither inferred nor postulated, but seen staying in position as we move about them, or moving and turning as we stand and look at them. The supposed inference or postulate is peculiar among inferences and postulates in that no one can ever remember having made it. But everyone who sees, actually sees things in depth, and sees the places beyond them from which he could see their hidden sides.

In the Humean type of doctrine, the perception of sensation as given is in a peculiar sense a pure perception or sensation. Just as shape and size were nothing but shape and size, colour was nothing but colour. The qualities of colour apart from the colour itself, so to speak, were removed: coldness, warmth, harshness, richness, gaiety, mellowness, limpidity. All these values were theoretically absent from the colour sensation as given. Furthermore, though colour was always extended, it was never admitted that it always had a texture, for texture was tactual and had to be explained by association. Colour was colour and nothing else. Red could have no look but red. It could not be angry or fiery, nor advance as blue receded. Thus the hypostatised appearance or look did not even correspond to the look of things but was an abstraction from it, for fieriness of colour like elegance of shape corresponded to nothing in the external causes of the stimulus.

But everything that had been taken out of perception had to be somehow accounted for. Synaesthesia was ascribed to the mechanism of association and subsidiary unverifiable hypotheses invoked to accomplish this. Other aspects of perceptual experience were ascribed to a secondary mechanism, the mechanism of pain, pleasure and the passions, which external sensation brought into play. Apart from bodily pain, however, pain and pleasure were not sensations; sensations were pleasant or painful but pleasure and pain were not sensations. What could they be? The answer was qualities or properties of sensations. But all qualities or properties of anything were sensations or reducible to sensations. Pleasure and pain never acquired any proper place or status in the doctrine nor could they even be caused, for only the sensations or passions were caused and pleasure and pain were not sensations or passions.

For actual experience and the analysis of it had been substituted a hypothetical system which would at best explain how it arose originally, though this could never be verified. But Hume, like so many of his successors, purports to be describing our actual experience, and of course he often does so – when he forgets his system or continues to say what he wants to say in spite of it. He happily ignores it when need be. As a *moraliste*, Hume makes his often acute observations in the ordinary language. They thus stand and fall quite independently of his theory of the passions. The illustrations of the mechanism of sympathy are a case in point; they may stand though one reject the mechanism.

The passions in Hume's theory arise from the sensations, which must come first: percept before affect, as in some versions of the modern stimulus-response theory. There is no basis in experience for this assertion of the causal priority of the percept. The examination of experience reveals something quite different: that perception is affective through and through and all the time.

CHAPTER NINE

AFFECTIVITY AND VALUE

To see is to look at something, to make it the figure in its contextual background. One notices, looks at, one thing or group of things rather than another ; or one thing catches one's attention rather than another. Why? Why does one look at one thing rather than another? Why does something catch one's attention? To say it is interesting is to say one is interested, at least for the moment. What is bizarre, striking, lovely, anomalous, huge or ugly, for example, is interesting. One is interested, struck, arrested, puzzled, melted, frozen, bewildered, repelled, attracted, at ease or on edge. But there is no ready-made or standard epithet for most of the things which are interesting or for the ways in which one is interested. One's long-term interests of course lead one to notice some things rather than others, but the sense of " interest " I am after is the more general one, which also includes casual, short-term, idle and momentary interest.

Bangs and flashes force one's attention willy-nilly, producing the " startle effect " as it is called. So also a push in the back or a bang on the head produces effects on us, or even someone waving a hand in front of our face. In these cases we are acted upon rather than acting. They are to looking and listening as being thrown is to leaping. But looking, listening and touching are exploratory and selective. What I want to suggest is that selectivity is affectivity and its correlate is value. My aim is limited to making a few essential points about the passions, emotions, feelings and sentiments and about values; any treatment in my revised terms of the moral values with which Hume is largely concerned is beyond the scope of this work.

Selection is preferential, visually as in other ways. What we notice is what is noticeable, what is worth a look. Sometimes, as in a dentist's waiting-room, one is not looking for anything in particular; one's eye lights on one thing and another – perhaps a picture, a calendar, or a chair is curious or intriguing, but not the wallpaper or the carpet or curtains. At other times, one wants to find out something and only what is relevant to that is of interest. Scenes and situations are perceived in terms of our purposes and preoccupations and desires.

I use the terms "affective" and "affectivity" rather than "emotion", "passion" and "feeling", because they include not only the meanings of these commoner words but also the continual ebb and flow of one's curiosity, interest, delight, desire, satisfaction, dissatisfaction, irritation and so on. When one is calmly at work – writing, say – there is no range of standard terms for the phases of the ebb and flow. It may be mild or it may be more strenuous. When, for example, one is having to struggle to express an argument, one feels tension, hope, disgust, despair. But when one is moving smoothly on, one is not in the ordinary sense feeling emotions, but one is calmly pleased with the way it is going, and this undisturbed feeling of progress and achievement is no less affective. The way we apprehend the present stage of a task as incomplete, muffed, muddled, or coming along, shaping up, lightening, is the way we feel about it, the way it looks to us, and of course a task is only a task to us, to someone, to a potential doer. The requiredness as we apprehend it is the correlate of our project and they cannot be separated. Our situation is the way we see it; it is a situation only for us, ordered and organised in relation to our desires, projects, and interests with potentialities and promising features, obstacles and barriers. It is in terms of our being in the world as an embodied consciousness that feeling, emotion or affectivity have to be understood.

Though Hume seems to start from the view that there is a definite range of distinctive, nameable passions, he realises in effect that these are only the more striking and overt phases of affectivity. He does suppose that the passions are caused by perceptions and indeed that they are themselves secondary perceptions. I wish to maintain that perception – in my sense: hearing, touching and seeing – is affective in the first place, through and through, and that the correlate of affectivity is value, at the perceptual as well as at other, or " higher ", levels. Hume supposes that the passion is an observable, identifiable occurrence, since it is a sensation or impression; though it only occurs in certain circumstances it would be what it is in any circumstances, its relation to other impressions being merely the relation of external association. But no such passion " itself" can be found. Feeling is someone's feeling about something in a situation; it is inseparable from what may be expressed as a value predicate of the object. But it is distinguishable, as the consciousness of the object is to be distinguished from the object of consciousness.

If the passion " itself " is not to be found, how do we know we are angry, for example, or delighted or afraid or uneasy?˙ The answer sometimes given is that we know this in the same way as we know that anyone else is angry, or delighted or afraid or uneasy – by observing the behaviour and symptoms which together constitute and define these different emotions. Though this view is finally untenable, the reasons which have led to its adoption are important and interesting. There are two main reasons.

In the first place, to know that one is angry, for example, to recognise it as anger, is to know the meaning of the word, to have a concept of anger, and to know when to use it. We learn the meaning of " anger " not simply from being angry but from being told we are angry or in a temper, from seeing others that we are told are angry, and from the reactions of others to our anger. Much the same goes for all the other passions – and for dispositions, propensities and character traits. In the second place, we can be angry without knowing it and others can know it long before we do – we may deny it angrily. To be angry is not to know one is angry, and the same goes for all the passions, emotions and feelings. Feeling is not to be identified with recognising, realising, knowing, or being aware of what we feel.

It is natural therefore to conclude that we recognise our own anger in the same way, or very nearly, as we recognise the anger of others: by the observable symptoms and behaviour. On this view, all that is missing in Hume's account is a description of the symptoms and behaviour in addition to what he gives an account of – the characteristic circumstances in which they occur. There would be no question of the passion " itself " as a further component. Anger would be a name for a certain range of observable symptoms and behaviour.

It would be reducible to overt, observable happenings. To know someone was angry would be to observe his flush or pallor, his trembling, glaring, shouting in a certain tone, to which might be added some physiological facts. To know that one was oneself angry would likewise be to observe these phenomena or some of them. Anger would thus be a state of a certain kind of object, the kind known as a person or, paradoxically, a subject.

In behaviourist descriptions, the observer or describer is left out of account. If he were not, he would not be observing but observed. But since the assumption is that only what is observed, objects, can be meaningfully spoken of or described, there are in effect no subjects but only objects, no selves but only others, no observers but only what is observed. Thus one knows one is angry in the same way as one knows others are angry. This has, of course to be regarded as a loose way of talking; one should not say " one knows ", one should say: Subject *A* is observed to be angry by the same criteria as Subjects *B, C, D*, etc. " Subject " in this context means " object " – what is observed – though it seems to be applied only to human objects, not to rats or monkeys.

It is quite important to realise that this is not Hume's view of the matter, nor can his view be revised at all plausibly in this direction. For Hume, the passion itself was not the situation or the circumstances in which it occurred, nor yet the externally observable behaviour and symptoms (which would of course for Hume be reducible to impressions of sensation). And to this extent I think Hume was right: to know what anger is, what it means to be angry, one must be angry or have been angry, just as to know what it means to see, one must see or have seen. Anger belongs to experience, consciousness, subjectivity. It is not a characteristic or reducible to characteristics of any observed object whatsoever, or, for example, to the chemical state of the bloodstream and similar criteria.

How then is it possible that, on the one hand, one may not know one is angry, and on the other, that one can tell when other people are angry? To be angry at someone for his conduct is to see him or think of him as mean, or disgraceful, or disobliging, or dishonest, or heartless, or irresponsible, or infuriating. It is to see or think of him angrily. We are not seeing or thinking *and* being angry. Our seeing

69

and thinking is angry, or our anger is the way we see or think of the odious, outrageous object of our anger. To be angry at is to be conscious of – to see, imagine, think of, have in mind – in a certain way. We may not know we are angry, may not realise or recognise our anger, because our attention is absorbed in the infuriating object of our anger. The sense in which we may be said not to know we are angry is the sense in which we may be said not to know we are seeing it or thinking of it: the consciousness of the object is in this case non-reflexive. But as our seeing it is implicit in its present visibility, so is our anger in its infuriatingness and all the implicitly anger-making predicates we might ascribe to it. But we can be reflexively aware of seeing someone or something and of being angry at him. We recognise we would love to clout him, but we are observing, looking at, perceiving only him; we cannot perceive our perceiving, nor perceive our desire to clout him. But we know we do perceive him and that we have a strong desire to clout him. In this sense of "know", knowing is not objective or based on observation of the patient's symptoms. The object of our anger remains the object, even as we become aware of our anger, or our feeling and attitude towards him.

But as we see with our eyes, bodily from where we are, so we are also bodily angry. We glare, clench our teeth and our fists perhaps, go hot or cold, shout, adopt a bodily attitude. When we become aware of this, we are still not perceiving or observing as we might someone else's clenched fists and much more. For we are our body: we know that our fists are clenched, that we are glaring furiously, that our cheeks are hot, without any observation of fists, eyes, or cheeks. And I need hardly repeat that we are not aware of any physiological effect or occurrence, though if we know some physiology we shall know that such effects are in operation.

Anger is not voluntary; that is why it is called a passion, or used to be called a passion. But we live it, assume it, suffer it, act it out, or suppress it. It is not a third person, objective process or series of occurrences. We can be as it were possessed, but we let ourselves be, let ourselves go, let it rip. To give it rein, to throw a fit, represents a choice of conduct; we do not lose control, we abandon ourselves to it, act it out. If we were not reflexively aware of being angry, the notions of self-control and restraint or lack of them would be meaningless. To act calmly, unclench the fists, breathe more deeply is already to be less angry. To do otherwise is to be angrier – to work oneself up.

Because we are bodily angry, or glad, sad, merry, etc., and may not know it, James's paradox may seem persuasive: we are sad because we weep or merry because we laugh. The ordinary view regards the feeling as prior to the expression; James's view reverses the order and it arises out of his dualism. For James, until he launched his attack on the concept of consciousness, the body was simply the organism, the object of physiology, and a bodily event was simply a physiological event. One's own bodily sensations and feelings were all events in consciousness, causally connected with physiological occurrences and processes. A self or subject, that is to say, was not a body. Hence weeping could *happen* and make us feel sad.

But our experience, as I have tried to argue, is essentially as embodied subjects. We are embodied or, if you like, we are our bodies. In experience, feeling may precede expression or they may be simultaneous, but both are bodily. To weep is to be sad, to assume one's sadness, not to snap out of it, to surrender to tears, to indulge one's feeling: again it is a choice of conduct. If we don't want to, we don't need to. Every feeling has its bodily expression, its expression in conduct, its range of possible developments. Feeling and expression are best conceived as matter and form: they are not separable, for the matter is expressed in the form, as what we mean is in the words we use and has no separate existence. Willy-nilly, we express our feelings and attitudes in posture, gesture, and face, if not in words. Not to express them is to suppress them.

One of the reasons most often advanced for a behaviourist account of how one knows one is angry or joyful is simply that sometimes one is, but does not know it, while others do know it. This view is, I think, reinforced by saying that one is then unconsciously angry or unconscious of one's anger. To be consciously angry is to realise one is angry, to be unconsciously angry is not to realise it. But it does not follow from this English idiom that we know we are angry from objective symptoms and behaviour, or that anger is primarily a name for an observable state of a subject or for a kind of behaviour. Tacitly assumed in this kind of account is the disembodied observer who is not what is observed – the signs, symptoms and behaviour – but who apprehends and interprets the bodily sensations and manifest movements, identifying empirically and inductively the state of anger in "subjects" which are more properly called objects.

The ghost that haunts this and similar views is the disembodied epistemological subject; anger is reduced to events in the third person. Anger is not a feeling, a passion – though no doubt there are feelings and sensations – but an objective, factual state of an object. Just as you tell that water is boiling by the bubbles and steam, so you tell that the kind of thing called a person is angry by his red face, loud voice, violent gestures and glaring eyes, etc., and these and other symptoms are all that anger is. That is what "anger" means. Anger is simply a compendious way of referring to a collection of associated phenomena. One may, though one need not, add the physiological description, as one might add the physical in the case of the water. Thus when I say I am angry I mean that this thing is in a publicly observable state.

On this view no one would actually feel angry and nothing would be experienced as infuriating. Subjectively one could never actually be angry or at least one could never know it. To know it, one would have to observe the thing, the object, the so-called self.

The common English idiom in which one is said to be consciously or unconsciously angry, conscious or unconscious of one's anger, by no means implies such a view. It is another way of making the distinction between realising and not realising that one is angry. But one does not observe the signs and identify them collectively as constituting anger. We become reflexively aware of being angry, as we become reflexively aware of seeing or hearing or thinking. As one can be said to be unconsciously angry, so one could be said to be unconsciously seeing something, or hearing or thinking. Most seeing is in this sense unconscious, that is to say, we are not reflexively aware of seeing something. What is meant by consciousness in this context is the reflexive consciousness, or self-consciousness.

Non-reflexively, however, seeing is essentially conscious, a consciousness of something. And to be angry is to be angrily conscious of, to experience angrily, to see angrily, think angrily, etc. Reflexion is the realisation of one's experience or consciousness of something, of one's attitude, feelings, emotions, passions. Without it, these words would refer to nothing whatsoever. Reflexion or self-consciousness is perfectly normal and commonplace, not something that only phenomenologists go in for. But some accounts of it are certainly misleading.

It is often spoken of as a consciousness of being conscious, as if the being conscious were an object. But when we are, for example, reflexively aware of seeing something, if we were not effectively seeing something we could not be aware of seeing it. What we see does not cease to be the object, else we would not be seeing. We are aware of seeing just that thing, not nothing in particular. To be aware of its present visibility is to be aware of seeing it. The snare – one of many – into which one falls in talking about consciousness is that one ignores one's body. Bodily experience is not experience of a body as in, for example, the experience of seeing a table. One has to *be* a body to see a table. Bodily experience is the experience of being a body, of being embodied, incarnate. The reflexive consciousness or self-consciousness is not a consciousness of a pure, disembodied consciousness, but of an embodied incarnate consciousness. To be aware of seeing is to be aware of seeing with one's eyes, and of seeing that very thing over there and visible.

And similarly, to realise one is angry at someone is to become aware that one is tense, itching to clout him, glaring, exploding, and that one sees him as detestable, infuriating, and that, for example, one regards his expression as smug, evil and devious. One is aware, not just of him in a certain way, but of the way in which one is aware of him, of one's own attitude and relation to him. One is a body and this awareness is of bodily experience, of the way one is regarding the object of one's anger. This awareness is reflexive. It is perhaps useful to illustrate the point about reflexive and non-reflexive bodily experience – or, if you like, conscious and unconscious bodily experience – in an example which has nothing to do with the emotions specially.

As I write, I am sitting with the pressure of the chair under me, arms on the table, feet on the floor. Most of the time, I am not, as they say, conscious of this. But it is implicit in what I am doing – writing this.

At any moment, however, I can be conscious or reflexively aware of this, attending to the pressure, posture and movements I am making. Again, most of the time I am writing, I am not conscious of moving the pen over the paper – for I am thinking of what I am writing, what I want to say. But again at any moment I can be, and this is reflexive. Nor most of the time am I conscious of seeing the paper on which I write, for that would be distracting; I am of course seeing it and seeing what I write, but I am not reflexively aware of this. But at any moment I can be. Again, I am not conscious of drawing on my pipe (much less of breathing), nor of taking it in my hand and shifting it to the other side of my mouth. But again, I can be.

Now the English idiom I have referred to is a bit misleading. For while it is sometimes said, for example, of someone who is obviously in a rage that he is unconsciously angry, it is never said of anyone absorbed in a book that he is unconsciously holding the book at a suitable distance from his eyes or that he is unconsciously sitting in his chair, or of someone absorbed in writing that he is unconsciously pushing the pen across the paper. I contend that this idiom would be as appropriate in the one case as in the other. In the terms which I think are less confusing, reading and writing or standing are all conscious activities but not necessarily reflexively conscious. And similarly for the feelings, emotions, passions and attitudes – they are conscious but not necessarily reflexively conscious. Reflexion is not observation, at least not in the ordinary sense. It is only by *being a body* that one can observe anything from anywhere. To be aware of oneself is to be aware of the body one is. The only sense in which one can literally observe it is the sense in which one can see a certain amount of it – but no one is going to suggest that that is how we know what we feel.

One's body is in a sense *a priori*; being a body is the condition of experience of things and other people. One is a body and when one is angry at someone and regards him as infuriating, one is bodily angry. There is no more difficulty in being aware of this reflexively than there is in being aware of the pressure of the chair under one. One's anger is not a set of physiological facts: one is not physiological facts. But one is one's body and to be angry or joyful or merry is to be bodily angry or joyful or merry – how else should one grin or

74

laugh? When one is overcome with hilarity or mirth, it is the mirth that shakes one's body from stem to stern. If one had never been shaken with mirth one would never know what it was like, what mirth was. And so with anger and with all other emotions.

But all feeling and emotions and passions are ways in which one experiences situations, people and things, and what can be formulated as value predicates of these are the correlates of one's feelings – an awkward or trying or delightful situation, a boring person, a hideous object. When someone is scintillating, one is alert, eager, hanging on his words. And when someone is tedious, one droops wearily. But it is bodily that one is alert or drooping, for one is not a disembodied mind. Naturally we are not taking notice of our attitude and feeling most of the time – our attention is devoted to the object. But there is no difficulty in taking notice and being reflexively aware of what we feel.

The next question is how we know what others feel. I have suggested that feeling and its expression are best conceived as matter and form, not as cause and effect. We express our feelings and attitudes in posture, gesture and face, if not in words. We know what others feel because we see their expressions, postures, gestures and conduct. As Ryle remarks, there is no "causal divination reinforced by weak analogical argument". We do not infer the cause of the expression we see on people's faces when we want to know what they feel. The expression, the form, is the form of the matter. We, as it were, read their expressions. We do not infer from the words we see and hear what their meaning is: it is in the words as matter to form. When an expression is cryptic and we are puzzled, there is nothing to go by but the expression. When we cannot understand a sentence and try to interpret it, we are not inferring its cause. Nor are we when we do not know what someone's expression or attitude means or portends. Having understood it, however, we may well have to infer why the person in question is angry or sulky or sad, that is, what he is angry or sulky or sad about.

One of Hume's most celebrated dicta is "The minds of men are mirrors to one another". But he insists that "no passion of another discovers itself immediately to the mind". Passions are not expressed in people's faces or conduct, according to Hume, they are inferred from signs, the connection being established by association. These external signs have no expression, no look, for they are simply complex impressions of sensation and nothing more. Hume's mechanism of sympathy cannot account for how we come to see an expression on a face. How does the expression get into the face?

This question is akin to a more elementary question which a sensationalist or datum doctrine of perception must answer: how do the *other* qualities get into a colour? For a colour datum according to such doctrines is nothing but colour – not nice or nasty, not warm or cold, not glaring or garish or mellow, not full-bodied or sickly, not glowing nor bilious. It is, so to speak, pure colour, in a peculiar sense of " pure ". But pure colour in this sense is never actually seen, never given in experience. The concept belongs to physical theories of colour, from which of course values and qualities other than the colour itself have to be excluded. In a doctrine such as Hume's, colour in this sense is identified with the datum of our experience of colour. Hume never addresses himself to this problem, nor so far as I know do any of his successors who hold sense-datum theories. In Hume's doctrine of sympathy, the idea of a passion, which occurs by association with such observed circumstances as would occasion it in our experience, differs from the passion only in vivacity, and because others resemble us we in some measure feel their passion. But as a matter of fact we may read the anger in another's face without feeling angry in any degree at all, and we may do this even without knowing what he is angry about. What we feel ourselves is another matter entirely.

It remains to say a word about the projection theory of value – that values are projected on things by our feelings, or that values *are* projected feelings. If feelings are what I take them to be there is no sense in which they can possibly be projected on what the feeling is about. They are our feelings, not the feelings of what we have in view or in mind. But, it may be said, the qualities and values of things might still be projected *by* our feelings. The difficulty is to know what precisely this could mean. Would we, for example, see a colour, have a feeling and project, say, mellowness on the colour, invest the colour with mellowness? Or would we see a girl, have a feeling, and project the prettiness on her, or invest her wiggle with seduction? There is no doubt about the feelings or about what the feelings are about. But we are asked to suppose that somehow or other – in what sense is impossible to determine – the feeling is prior to the prettiness. The origins of this theory lie in the sensation or datum view of perception: what is given is colour, size and shape and nothing else. The hypostatised look of a thing or person is a look from which the values have been extracted.

But, as I have said, we see things the way we see them and they look the way they look. As an objectively determinable object, a girl is not pretty, for to regard her as such is to ignore her looks.

CHAPTER TEN

THINGS IN THE WORLD

ONE of Hume's purposes in Parts 3 and 4 of Book I is to refute the doctrine of representative perception, to deny the double existence, representing and represented. Always at the back of his mind and sometimes in the forefront, however, is the physical and physiological theory which led to the doctrine of representative perception, the doctrine of sense-impressions – affections of the external sense organs, conveyed by the nerves and animal spirits, and causing conscious sensations in the mind. These, he asserts repeatedly, are known to us by consciousness as they really are. But his whole doctrine of the senses is founded on the theory and has no foundation in actual experience. The point may be illustrated in his accounts of taste and smell and of solidity.

If anyone says that he experiences a sound or smell as filling a room, Hume's reply is: you cannot, for these are impressions, arising from the senses, internal and perishing existences, and are in the mind. But, probably realising the difficulty, he never asserts that the smell is in one's nose or the sound in one's ears. He prefers to assert that they are nowhere

> . . . and I assert, that this is not only possible, but the greatest part of things do and must exist after this manner. An object may be said to be nowhere, when its parts are not so situated with respect to each other, as to form any figure or quantity; nor the whole with respect to other bodies so as to answer to our notions of contiguity or distance. Now this is evidently the case with all our perceptions and objects, except those of sight and feeling. A moral reflection cannot be plac'd on the right or on the left hand of a passion, nor can a smell or a sound be either of a circular or a square figure. These objects and perceptions, so far from requir-

78

ing any particular place, are absolutely incompatible with it, and even the imagination cannot attribute it to them. . . . 'Twill not now be necessary to prove, that those perceptions, which are simple, and exist nowhere, are incapable of any conjunction in place with matter or body, which is extended and divisible; since 'tis impossible to found a relation but on some common quality. . . . Thus supposing we consider a fig at one end of a table, and an olive at the other, 'tis evident, that in forming the complete ideas of these substances, one of the most obvious is that of their different relishes; and 'tis as evident, that we incorporate and conjoin these qualities with such as are colour'd and tangible. The bitter taste of the one, and sweet of the other are supposed to lie in the very visible body, and to be separated from each other by the whole length of the table. This is so notable and so natural an illusion, that it may be proper to consider the principles, from which it is derived.

(Treatise, p. 235)

Hume argues that this conjunction in place of the taste, smell and colour is a relation added by the mind to supplement the relation of contiguity in the time of their appearance. But there is no more reason to say the taste is nowhere than to say the colour is nowhere. Taste is not colour, but the parallel between them holds to this extent that just as you do not see the colour of the fig when you are not looking at it, so you do not feel or taste the savour of the fig when you are not eating it. Hume's rhetorical question whether the taste is in every part of the fig or only in some, simply establishes what we all know, that taste is different from colour, not that the taste is not the taste of the fig as the colour is the colour of the fig. You taste the fig in your mouth: it has to be there for you to taste it. When it is in your mouth you cannot see it, but Hume would not argue that then the taste is somewhere but the colour nowhere. It would, however, be just as plausible to do so.

Hume simply forgets that it is only by virtue of one's body that one has any experience of figs at all, that in order to perceive anything anywhere one has to be somewhere bodily oneself. His references to the senses are entirely unintelligible apart from the body, which is itself extended and in depth and is so experienced. But his argument depends on the disembodiment of the senses.

In his argument on the primary and secondary qualities in Book 1, Part 4, Section iv, Hume's main point is that the primary cannot be apprehended without the secondary. But it is in this section that the primacy of the visual for Hume becomes explicit, a primacy which is of fundamental importance in his analysis of causality. He argues that we can have no idea of solidity independently of a visible extension on the ground that the impressions of touch are simple impressions, and the feeling is quite different from the solidity. This argument is close to the one concerning taste, and Hume might say equally well that the sensation of touch was nowhere. Yet to make this point he takes the body for granted: " An object, that presses upon any of our members, meets with resistance; and that resistance, by the motion it gives to the nerves and animal spirits, conveys a certain sensation to the mind; but it does not follow, that the sensation, motion, and resistance are any ways resembling." (*Treatise*, p. 230.) His argument is of course directed against the standard theory. But he is entirely the victim of it, and cursorily rejects the experience of feeling something, touching something, exploring something with the hand, pressing, grasping, etc., in favour of what really, according to the theory, happens – sensations in the mind, nowhere.

He is to explain how we believe in bodies on the basis of a doctrine which would be inconceivable without bodies, notably the human body and sense organs, and which requires him to regard actual experience as somehow illusory, yet at the same time to assert bravely that of what we are most intimately conscious we cannot be mistaken – impressions. If Hume had taken Berkeley seriously, he would have realised that the body, the organism, the nerves and animal spirits are in the same boat as the other alleged external objects: they too have to be mere perceptions and it cannot be as a result of their independent operation that we have perceptions, for that would be to accept the theory of the double existence, representing and represented, the perceptions and the real physical body.

Hume recognises the difficulty at various points, but he does not overcome it, for he continues to refer to the senses and sense organs, directly and indirectly, though these expressions have no meaning apart from eyes and ears and hands and skin, from seeing, hearing, touching and moving. The " experiments " whereby he proves that our perceptions are "not possest of any distinct or independent existence" are experiments with bodies: "When we press one eye with a finger, we immediately perceive all the objects to become double. . . ." (*Treatise*, pp. 210–11.) Are the finger and the eye perceptions? Not for the moment. They are what we perceive the objects (or perceptions) with, parts of the body in fact. At other times, the finger and the eye and all the rest of the body are mere perceptions too. But they are nevertheless perceived with " the senses ": "Properly speaking, 'tis not our body we perceive . . . but certain impressions, which enter by the senses. . . ." (*Treatise*, p. 191.) Even as Hume tries to reduce the body to impressions " on the same footing " with any other impression, there have to be senses and sense organs, a real body, for there to be any impressions at all, and this requires the double existence, representing and represented. Though his every argument that the immediate object of consciousness is an impression is derived from a consideration of the body, Hume insists all the more strongly that the impressions are " known to us by consciousness "; what we call the body therefore can only consist of such impressions. What we are immediately aware of is what, according to the physiological theory, we *must* be aware of; but if so, the body itself must be so reducible.

The theory is thus circular: the doctrine of impressions is the outcome of a study of the body, but the body is itself reducible to impressions. The " we " to whom the impressions " must necessarily appear in every particular what they are, and be what they appear ", is a disembodied consciousness; that is all " we " can be if the body be reduced to "our" perceptions. And so it is in most of Hume's frequent references to the mind or consciousness and its activities. But he never makes this explicit and continually falls back upon embodiment without realising it. How can a disembodied mind, which can itself be nowhere, have a "propensity to spread itself on external objects " as his doctrine of causality requires? How can an impression be "an internal and perishing existence"? Internal or external to what? There is only one answer: the body.

It is the disembodied mind, however, which Hume attempts to be quit of in his celebrated account of personal identity. The mind or self is composed of perceptions and "identity is nothing really belonging to these different perceptions, and uniting them together; but is merely a quality, which we attribute to them, because of the union of their ideas in the imagination, when we reflect upon them." (*Treatise* p. 260.) Who are the "we" who reflect upon them and what is the "imagination"? There is only one answer: the disembodied consciousness. Again, as in the case of the body, Hume tries to have it both ways, assuming and denying; we are conscious of our perceptions, perceptions are in the mind or imagination, but the mind is nothing but perceptions; it is composed of perceptions.

His account of the self follows the nature of the perception as he conceives it. To recapitulate: firstly, the perception is both object and consciousness, but secondly, it is itself an object of consciousness. Firstly, the mind is composed of perceptions, but secondly, perceptions are united in the mind or imagination, and "we" reflect upon them. Hume's account of relations requires the latter view: they are known by intuition or comparison, but it is not the terms of the relation which intuit or compare.

Throughout Book I, Hume's concrete examples all refer to things, not perceptions. Now things, according to Hume's analysis in Part 4, are fictitious identities of the imagination. In Husserlian terms, they are meant or intended unities or identities, noemata. Either this is an analysis of what the vulgar mean by a thing or it is pointless. What Hume is indeed accounting for is the distinction, for example, between the table and my seeing the table from different angles yesterday, today and tomorrow, which is the vulgar distinction. The table is the identity, the seeings of it are not. For the vulgar, the table is the object, not the seeing or imagining or thinking of. Hume of course knows this: "When we are absent from it, we say it still exists, but that we do not feel it, we do not see it." (*Treatise*, p. 207.) What he means by a perception is not the thing which we suppose to exist independently of our seeing or feeling it. Yet Hume insists that the vulgar take their perceptions to be their only objects. This is simply not so. Perceptions correspond to the different appearances of things, the different views one has of them, and Hume in effect makes this very point in his reference to the " seeming encrease and diminution of objects, according to their distance; by the apparent alterations in their figure; by the changes in their colour and other qualities from our sickness and distempers; and by an infinite number of other experiments of the same kind; from all which we learn, that our sensible perceptions are not possest of any distinct or independent existence " (*Treatise*, p. 211). The point Hume is making is amply made in the vulgar parlance; it is quite simply the distinction between the thing and the way I see it now from here. To say that the vulgar take their perceptions to be their only objects is on the face of it to say that the vulgar do not make the distinction. But they do. The thing that I see now from here can be seen from other places, in other lights and circumstances – it has other sides. That is what we mean by a table or chair or hat or shoe: that sort of thing.

What leads Hume to give his peculiar and misleading account of the vulgar consciousness? He is fighting on two fronts. He wants to give a critique of the vulgar consciousness, but he is intent on refuting the doctrine of representative perception. In rejecting the double existence, however, it is not the representation he rejects but what it represents – the real physical object. Perceptions are intra-mental entities, and strictly internal and perishing existences. But in his polemic against the philosophical view, Hume treats them as representations, simulacra of the real thing, though they represent nothing and there is no real thing. Perceptions are all there is, or at least all we can know there is. Hence he is led into saying that the vulgar take their perceptions to be their only objects. He is himself the victim of the philosophical view and takes his only objects to be perceptions. What the vulgar take to be objects – things – can only on his view be perceptions.

That I may avoid all ambiguity and confusion on this head, I shall observe, that here I account for the opinions and beliefs of the vulgar with regard to the existence of body; and therefore must entirely conform myself to their manner of thinking and of expressing themselves. Now we have already observ'd, that however philosophers may distinguish betwixt the objects and perceptions of the senses; which they suppose co-existent and resembling; yet this is a distinction, which is not comprehended by the generality of mankind, who as they perceive only one being, can never assent to the opinion of a double existence and representation. Those very sensations, which enter by the eye or ear, are with them the true objects, nor can they readily conceive that this pen or paper, which is immediately perceiv'd, represents another, which is different from, but resembling it. In order, therefore, to accommodate myself to their notions, I shall at first suppose; that there is only a single existence, which I shall call indifferently *object* or *perception*, according as it shall seem best to suit my purpose, understanding by both of them what any common man means by a hat, or shoe, or stone, or any other impression, convey'd to him by his senses. I shall be sure to give warning, when I return to a more philosophical way of speaking and thinking.

(*Treatise*, p. 202)

Hume has of course repeatedly followed the terminology which he here somewhat portentously announces as conforming to the vulgar manner. The ambiguity and confusion which he tries to avoid is simply made worse. What any common man means by a hat or shoe is not what Hume means by an impression, those very sensations which enter by the eye or ear. If that were so, " impression " and " thing " would be synonyms. But a thing is not the seeing of it. It need not be seen to be: it is not an internal and perishing existence. To call the single existence indifferently *object* or *perception* is not to accommodate himself to the vulgar belief at all: it is simply to confuse the issue. What corresponds to a perception in the vulgar parlance is not the thing, but the way the thing looks to me here and now, the look of the thing; things can be seen from different places at different times in different lights; furthermore, they can be handled, explored, examined, submitted to test and experiment, and this is the most obvious sense in which they are independent – their pecularities are discovered, not invented. But for Hume this is not a problem at all: the problem of independent existence is reduced to the problem of continued existence when they are unperceived. And this follows from his identification, foisted upon the vulgar, of perceptions and things.

> 'Tis certain, that almost all mankind, and even philosophers themselves, for the greatest part of their lives, take their perceptions to be their only objects. . . . 'Tis also certain, that this very perception or object is supposed to have a continu'd uninterrupted being, and neither to be annihilated by our absence, nor to be brought into existence by our presence. When we are absent from it, we say it still exists, but that we do not feel, we do not see it.
>
> (*Treatise*, p. 207)

Hume's question is how a perception can exist unperceived, and his premise is that what we suppose we see or perceive is really a perception. A table, for example, is a perception. He is asking how we suppose that " the interruption in the appearance of a perception implies not necessarily an interruption in its existence ". The confusion is only explicable if one bears in mind that he is attacking the representative theory, and that of the double existence he has retained the representation, the simulacrum-table in the mind. This he takes to be what is ordinarily meant by " the table ", and since it is only a representation or perception one may speak of the interruption in the appearance of the perception just as one may talk of the interruption in the appearance of the table.

He ignores the fact that what we call a table is in depth while what he calls a perception is two-dimensional, flat. The perception-table would be more like a picture of a table. But he forgets about this during his discussion of the broken appearances and how we unite them. United or not, they would still all be flat, for Hume never explains how a third dimension gets into the picture. The alleged perplexity arising from the broken appearances is entirely Hume's. His problem is not, for example, how I believe that the book which I see continues to exist when I am not looking at it, but in effect how I

85

believe an appearance to exist when it is not appearing, not an appearance, to which the vulgar, and only, answer is: I don't. But this is
what he makes out that the vulgar do believe.

Even his account of the philosophical view is obscured thereby.
By way of correcting the vulgar opinion, he remarks " that all our
perceptions are dependent on our organs . . . from all which we learn,
that our sensible perceptions are not possest of any distinct or independent existence" (*Treatise*, p. 211). But this *is* the vulgar opinion: it
amounts to saying that we do not see things when we are not looking
at them, i.e. when they do not appear, and that they look different at
different times. He continues:

> The natural consequences of this reasoning shou'd be, that our
> perceptions have no more a continu'd than an independent exis-
> tence; and indeed philosophers have so far run into this opinion,
> that they change their system, and distinguish (as we shall do for
> the future) betwixt perceptions and objects, of which the former
> are supposed to be interrupted, and perishing, and different at
> every return; the latter to be uninterrupted, and to preserve a
> continu'd existence and identity.

What Hume is here describing is prima facie more like the vulgar view,
which makes the distinction between the table which has a continued
existence and identity, and my seeing the table at different times and in
different ways, and which is embodied in the very language. Having
radically misrepresented the vulgar view, Hume then attributes something very like it to the learned.

All right, it may be said, Hume has been careless in his exposition,
but after all he does give an account of the vulgar, natural belief in the
independent continuing existence of things. In the end, the thing –
hat, shoe or stone – is the identity, the fiction of the imagination. What
he is accounting for in the end is the vulgar belief, and is it not a
plausible account?

It is plausible certainly in the sense that we do all believe in the
continuing independent existence of things. But I see no reason to
suppose that Hume has been careless in his exposition in any material
respect. The confusion about what a perception is, the ambiguity of

the concept, is central to his whole doctrine, and forces him to say the conflicting and contradictory things he does say. His account of the belief in the world and all the continuing things in it is inseparable from this confusion. For Hume, we arrive at the belief through the experience of contradiction and perplexity at the broken appearances, and seek relief in the fiction from our uneasiness at the conflict between the identity of the resembling perceptions and the interruption of the appearance. Hume is forced into this fairy story by his premises which are derived entirely from the learned doctrine that the immediate objects of the mind are its own representations or perceptions. This masquerades as an account of our actual experience, and he insists repeatedly that these perceptions are known as such by consciousness.

An account of experience must take it as it is, not as one might suppose on the basis of a physical or physiological doctrine that it must be, or must originally be. We have no experience except as embodied beings. The belief in the continued existence of things would hardly be possible for beings which did not have experience of things external to and independent of themselves, which they could approach and examine and discover more and more about: what one discovers in this way is experienced as being there already – we don't invent it. Again, I could not believe that there is a wall behind my back if I had no back, nor that there are things elsewhere if I were not here, that is to say if I were not a body. Nor could I believe that things exist unperceived if I did not see them in depth, for to see something in depth is to see it as having another unseen side which I could see from a vantage point beyond, for I can also move, and I can see where I could move to. An embodied being is always somewhere, and where he is is identified only in relation to where he has been, will be or could be, to other places where there are other things. To say I am here and now is to say there is a world in space and time. When I move to another place it would not be *another* place if there were not a place I had left.

It never occurred to Hume and it has occurred to few if any of the commentators that so far as perceptions are concerned some of the commonest adverbs and prepositions and place words would be unintelligible: up, down, over, under, behind, before, left, right, top, bottom. All these words could have meaning only for an embodied being, situated and oriented in the world. For a disembodied consciousness its perceptions could not have a top or bottom, a left side or a right side – these expressions would be meaningless. This escapes notice only because Hume secretly supposes that the disembodied consciousness sees, i.e. that it is embodied, as his inconsequent references to the internal and external show, as well as his references to the senses.

Again and again, Hume's argument is plausible because he, and with him the reader, tacitly assumes what he has no right to assume. For example, he says: " To begin with the *senses*, 'tis evident these faculties are incapable of giving rise to the notion of the *continued* existence of their objects after they no longer appear to the senses. For that is a contradiction in terms, and supposes that the senses continue to operate, even after they have ceas'd all manner of operation." (*Treatise*, p. 188.) If one forgets that " object " here means " perception ", one may easily fail to notice Hume's confusion of the object of the senses in the ordinary sense – the thing we see – and the perception or impression which results from the stimulation of the senses, and therefore suppose that Hume is merely saying that a thing is not seen when it is not seen, or that we do not see it when we do not see it. Hume insouciantly trades on the normal meaning of " object of the senses " and then produces an argument which identifies this with the perception. But the doctrine of perceptions as internal and perishing existences presupposes the body, the external sense organs, the nerves and animal spirits. The only way to avoid the charge of circularity, of assuming the findings of a science of the body to explain the belief in bodies, is to assert as he does " that all sensations are felt by the mind, such as they really are ".

When made explicit, his argument requires, for example, that what is ordinarily described as seeing a table should be known as it really is, as a complex impression of sensation, in the flat and nowhere. He insists that what is really given, the immediate object, is the perception. But of course we do see tables and chairs and that sort of thing. So tables and chairs are perceptions. Having thus identified the alleged external object and the intramental entity, he has disposed of external and distinct existence, and his only problem is that of continuing existence to which independent existence is reduced: " If our senses, therefore, suggest any idea of distinct existences, they must convey the impressions as those very existences by a kind of fallacy and illusion." (*Treatise*, p. 189.)

When he comes to examine the question why we attribute a distinct and continued existence to some impressions and not to others and finds they have " a peculiar constancy ", his examples are " mountains, and houses, and trees, which lie at present under my eye ". They " change not upon account of any interruption in my seeing or perceiving them ". All quite true, and the reader readily accepts this if he forgets that he is required to hold that what he sees are perceptions: that is the whole point of the argument. The same goes for the subsequent and celebrated passage in which Hume, seated in his chamber, describes the reflexions and reasonings occasioned by the entry of a porter with a letter from a friend 200 leagues distant (*Treatise*, p. 196). The reader may again very readily forget the point: things, the porter and all are perceptions. So is what would commonly be called Hume – the large man sitting in the chamber. The " I " of the narrative cannot strictly be anywhere, or if the " I " be nothing but the perceptions, it *is* also the porter, the letter, the friend, and everything else it would commonly be said to think of or imagine. In another passage of the same kind (*Treatise*, p. 199), Hume ignores the paradox in his terms of talking of the perception *of* the sun or ocean, when the sun and ocean *are* perceptions, and reduces the question of the continued existence of the perceptions to the continued existence of the sun or ocean. The question is continuously begged: the world and the things in it are taken as premises of an argument which is supposed to show how we believe in things and a world continuously existing, when all we have is perceptions, internal and perishing existences.

CHAPTER ELEVEN

BODY AND CAUSALITY

" WE may well ask *What causes induce us to believe in the existence of body?* but 'tis in vain to ask, *Whether there be body or not?* That is a point which we must take for granted in all our reasonings." (*Treatise*, p. 187.)

Does Hume mean that we must take for granted the existence of body to account for our belief in it? Or does he simply mean that the question whether there be body or not is unanswerable, and the only question is how we come to believe there is body? The latter is the usual interpretation, borne out by his analysis of bodies as fictitious identities of the imagination. But I am not sure that this is all Hume means. The above quotation can be read as a recognition by Hume that his argument is circular, that he takes the existence of body for granted in giving a causal account of our belief in body. It seems to me clear that he does do this, and the question is whether he recognises what he is doing. His account of the belief in the causal relation is so flagrantly a causal account that he can hardly have failed to recognise it; this seems to me to enhance the possibility that he explicitly intends to assume the existence of body as well as causality in accounting for the belief in body.

The question is a fundamental one for the whole interpretation of Hume's philosophy. If he were taking body and causality for granted in accounting for the beliefs in body and necessary connection, his account would be simply a " scientific " theory, which would leave the metaphysical and epistemological questions untouched. Now this tendency is inherent in his concept of human nature as a part of nature, and his Newtonian model of experiment and explanation. On this interpretation and only on this interpretation can Hume be said to give a psychological account of the belief in body and causality. In any of its modern meanings, psychology is intra-mundane: it is concerned with given creatures, animal or human, in the world, and takes these creatures in the world and causality for granted. It is, or intends to be, a science. There are great difficulties in this view of psychology which I shall discuss later in connection with Ryle's *The Concept of Mind*; the principal one concerns the reduction of subjectivity, experience, to objective, causal explanation. But my point for the moment is simply that if Hume's account is psychological in the modern meaning, it must be one which takes the world and causality for granted, and cannot be an account of the world and causality as constituted by belief and imagination without circularity.

It is largely useless to ask what sort of account Hume intends to give, for he makes no explicit distinction between science and philosophy. Natural, moral and mental philosophy are distinguished by their subject matters and the peculiar difficulties which these respectively present. But they all deal with aspects of nature. Hume does suggest in his Introduction that the science of human nature is somehow fundamental: " 'Tis evident, that all the sciences have a relation, greater or less, to human nature; and that however wide any of them may seem to run from it, they still return back by one passage or another." (*Treatise*, p. xix.) They " lie under the cognizance of men, and are judged of by their powers and faculties ". But it is much more plausible to interpret this in modern terms as the assertion that psychology is the fundamental science than as an assertion that epistemology and moral philosophy are different in kind from any science.

Metaphysics for Hume was school metaphysics. Science, experiment, was the thing. But the fictions of the imagination, as he called them, are the things that science in the first place is about—bodies. But Hume never makes this point, and never recognises that his science of man is not a science like the others, but a First Philosophy, no less than Aristotle's, and that he speakes more truly than he knows when, in his attack on substance, he jokingly suggests that perceptions are substances. This is what for him they are – τά ὄντα, οὐσία.

In Hume's account of causality, as in his account of the belief in the existence of body, " object " means both " thing " and " perception ". Now, *ex hypothesi*, there is no intrinsic, causal or necessary connection between one impression or idea and another; each is as it is and as it appears, regardless of any other. The point about Hume's elaborate argument, however, is that the conclusion prescribed by the definition of impressions and ideas is applied to things. Furthermore, his account of the causal belief is a causal account. The causes of the causal belief are therefore either *real* causes, which could only be known by God, or they presuppose the causal belief, in which case his argument is circular.

If we take a bodily sensation as the type of an impression, which Hume invites us to do, it is evident that one sensation does not cause another sensation; nor does anyone suppose so. Tooth-decay causes toothache, but tooth-decay is not a sensation. A pin entering the skin causes a jab; the jab is a sensation but not the pin or the skin. Again, if we take as corresponding to what Hume means by a complex impression what I see as I see it from my window, or any particular thing – a house or a tree – the way I see it now, this view or appearance is not a cause or an effect of any other view. (On the causal theory of perception, of course, all the appearances are effects, but none of them is the cause of any other.) One appearance or look of a thing does not cause another appearance or look; they can never be more than successive, contiguous, and constantly conjoined. Looks, appearances, perceptions are not things, but hypostatised entities. One billiard ball causes another to move, but the look of the one does not cause the look of the other: the terms of the causal relation are the balls, not the looks, that is to say the causal relation is asserted between two identities, fictions of the imagination in Hume's terms, not between two impressions or ideas.

An analysis of causality is condemned to futility if it does not take as examples what we do regard as cases of cause and effect. Hume again does what he accuses the vulgar of doing, confounding perceptions and objects. But his analysis can only be significant in so far as it is concerned with the motions, actions and reactions, and changes of things, for these are what we take to be causes and effects. Hume calls an effect " an object which begins to exist ", and this expression reveals as clearly as anything his confusion: the object in this context is not what we call a thing, but a perception. When a stationary billiard ball begins to roll, a new perception begins to exist, in Hume's terms. He nevertheless treats the new perception as if it were the thing. This is essential to his whole argument.

Now most of his argument is concerned with causal inference, inference from what is observed to its cause or effect on the basis of past experience. It is very little concerned with observation and experience as such, and with what we do observe and experience. The reason for this is that Hume has settled that matter *a priori*: all we can ever *really* observe or experience are contiguous and successive impressions. But he applies this dogma to bodies, things.

> Motion in one body is regarded upon impulse as the cause of motion in another. When we consider these objects with the utmost attention, we find only that the one body approaches the other; and that the motion of it precedes that of the other ; but without any sensible interval. 'Tis in vain to rack ourselves with *farther* thought and reflexion upon this subject. We can go no *farther* in considering this particular instance.
>
> (*Treatise*, pp. 76–7)

It is of course only if we take what is present to be a succession of impressions – which have paradoxically to be called visual – that we can go no farther. His argument requires one, though it is ostensibly about bodies, to be a purely visual observer, immobile, deaf, and preferably disembodied: that is the rule of the game. But there is no reason why we should play this artificial game.

There might be some point in it if Hume were really playing fair: but to play fair one must either stick to bodies or stick to perceptions. Hume has confused them and it is easy to show this. What is that word " impulse " doing in the passage quoted? It certainly applies to bodies. An impulse is a push; a push is the action of one thing on another and to say such action is causal is not to add anything. One must regard the phrase " upon impulse " as inadvertent on Hume's part. He means to deny that pushes can be observed, and to assert that only motion and change can be observed. But if I put my finger in front of a moving billiard ball or cannon ball I feel the ball pushing my finger and see what I feel. Hume or any sensationalist would instantly deny this: you cannot see what you feel. But in doing so he has to talk about sensations and impressions, not about things, not about billiard balls or cannon balls. Indeed one cannot properly talk about seeing or feeling, though one must; it is done with the words " visual " and " tactual ". To insist with the sensationalist that I cannot see what I feel – the push of the ball – is to say that I cannot feel with the hand that I see the billiard ball that I also see. Billiard balls and, in general, bodies are seen with one's eyes and felt with one's hands. What sort of billiard ball would it be that one could not both see and touch and be touched by? A Humean billiard ball, not really a billiard ball but a visual perception. A perception cannot give a push: there is absolutely no need for Hume to argue that point. But when he invites the reader to " consider these objects with the utmost attention " or " in themselves ", what he means is " as perceptions ".

Now pushes are causes, though it does not add anything to what we experience as a push to call it a cause. If I put my finger in front of the moving billiard ball, letting it dangle, I feel the push and it moves the finger: I feel it moving my finger, which is to say, causing my finger to move. To say it causes my finger to move is to say no more than that it moves my finger, and this is a matter of actual direct experience. Similarly when I push the ball, or pick it up and roll it, there is no point in saying I cause it to move, for that is merely a less explicit way of saying I push it or roll it. Passive and active pushes are just as much matters of experience as visible movements. All our experience is the experience of an embodied being; there are not two or three or more – a seeing one, a touching one, and a moving one – but one embodied being which sees, touches and moves. Thus I see the push as well as feel it, just as I see the roughness of a surface as well as the colour, or grasp the very thing which I see. We need not " rack ourselves " to know that we observe not merely two movements when one billiard ball rolls up to another, but the one hitting, pushing, impelling the other, which, if one wants to use the otiose word " cause ", means causing the other to move. There is no question of an occult cause. Pushes and pulls are matters of direct experience, just like colours. There is nothing occult about being jostled on a crowded bus or being dragged by a child towards the sweet-shop; one actually feels the push or the pull. Similarly one has direct experience of strength, force, power, resistance, weight in lifting, laying, hoisting, throwing and swinging things. One knows what force and power are by shoving and being shoved, just as one knows what colour is by seeing colours.

One does not experience one's own body as a thing, except to some extent when one contemplates it – for example, one's hand lying on the table. Even then, if one moves a finger it is only imperfectly a thing or object, for I, who see it, am moving (it), as I might move my eyes to see it. But apart from the occasions when I contemplate it in this way, it is entirely me, a subject not an object. It is by being a body that I have any experience of things, events, processes, phenomena. As a doer engaged in various tasks, my arms and hands are not things among other things but the power I have to reach, touch, grasp and manipulate things and are so experienced – non-thetically, as Sartre would say. They are not themselves things which one manipulates or grasps or moves or touches – for it is with them that one grasps, etc. To touch one's own hand is to touch it with one's other hand, and though normally touching and being touched are just as different from each other as are pushing and being pushed, in this case the experience is peculiar and ambiguous. Similarly, in action, one's legs are experienced as the power to get at, near, round about, over or away from things.

One does not move one's body; one moves bodily; movement is bodily movement. To move anything one must be a body, an embodied subject, and as such lift or heave or push or pull it. The one body one cannot lift or heave or push or pull is one's own, for even in climbing a rope or hoisting oneself on to a high wall it is as a body that one is pulling or hoisting. One has to say one lifts one's arms and use many similar expressions in order to specify what movement one is making. But it is easy to ignore the difference between lifting one's arm and lifting a hammer, say. One lifts the hammer with one's hand and arm, but one doesn't lift one's arm with anything, for it is a part of oneself, the embodied subject.

Hume's discussion of bodily movement in the Appendix (*Treatise*, p. 632) is founded on the distinction between a volition and a movement of the body. He insists that "the actions of the mind are, in this respect, the same with those of matter. We perceive only their constant conjunction: nor can we ever reason beyond it. No internal impression has an apparent energy, more than external objects have. Since, therefore, matter is confess'd by philosophers to operate by an unknown force, we shou'd in vain hope to attain an idea of force by consulting our own minds." To consult one's own mind in this context can only be to consult a disembodied mind, for Hume's argument is based straightforwardly on the mind–matter dualism; the body is matter and there is therefore no question of consulting one's experience as an embodied being – the experience of being a body – to attain the idea of force. Voluntary movement is held to consist in a mental volition followed by a movement of matter. But this is a theoretical construct required by dualist theory, not an analysis of the experience of doing and acting, in which the mental volition is not identifiable but pressure, resistance and force are. As Ryle has argued, to my mind conclusively, volitions belong to the theory of the ghost in the machine.

In the *Enquiry*, Hume discusses the question at greater length, but is prevented by his preconceptions from recognising the importance of the " animal nisus ", as he calls it. This " though it can afford no accurate precise idea of power, enters very much into that vulgar, inaccurate idea, which is form'd of it." (D. Hume, *Enquiry Concerning Human Understanding*, p. 67.) This point is consigned to a footnote, though one might have supposed that the vulgar idea of power was the very one, if not the only one, whose origin it was important to identify. But Hume's concern is causal inference and necessary connection and he of course identifies power and necessary connection.

Having found that external objects give us no idea of power or necessary connection:

Let us see [he says] whether this idea be derived from reflection on the operations of our own minds, and be copied from any internal impression. It may be said, that we are every moment conscious of internal power; while we feel, that, by the simple command of our will, we can move the organs of our body, or direct the faculties of our mind. An act of volition produces motion in our limbs, or raises a new idea in our imagination. This influence of the will we know by consciousness. . . . But the means, by which this is effected; the energy by which the will performs so extraordinary an operation; of this we are so far from being immediately conscious, that it must for ever escape our most diligent enquiry.

(Enquiry, pp. 64–5)

The terms in which Hume puts the problems are again those of the dualist theory of the interaction of soul and body, the body being the particular bit of matter on which the soul acts. The suggestion that we are every moment conscious of internal power, he interprets as meaning that we are conscious of the power of the mind or will, for embodied experience, the experience of being a body, is excluded from consideration. Just as my hand moves the pen, so my volitions move my hand; the connection is equally mysterious. Volitions are the "occult inner thrusts" of which Ryle speaks, like the thrust of my hand on a lever, except that they are unobservable. Hume takes them for granted, as he does the theory to which they belong, but not the actual experience of being a body. Hence he cites the case of a man struck with palsy who tries to move his limbs but cannot, and argues from this that neither in his case nor in the normal case "are we ever conscious of power". "Consciousness", he says, "never deceives."

But the whole passage is based on the assumption that we do not really have bodily experience, that our experience is that of pure minds associated with things which are mere things we can "command", but not really *us*. I don't know about the palsy, but what one experiences when one is too weak to move is weakness, bodily weakness; one tries to stand up but can't, but the trying is not the act of a disembodied mind; one tries bodily. This sort of experience is important for understanding what is meant by an act of will or sheer will-power and indeed the meaning of "can" and "cannot", as we shall see below. But Hume denies direct experience in favour of science:

We learn from anatomy, that the immediate object of power in voluntary motion, is not the member itself which is moved, but certain muscles, and nerves, and animal spirits, and, perhaps,

97

something still more minute and more unknown, through which the motion is successively propagated, ere it reach the member itself whose motion is the immediate object of volition. Can there be a more certain proof that the power, by which this whole operation is performed, so far from being directly and fully known by an inward sentiment or consciousness, is, to the last degree, mysterious and unintelligible? Here the mind wills a certain event: Immediately another event, unknown to ourselves, and totally different from the one intended, is produced: This event produces another, equally unknown: Till at last, through a long succession, the desired event is produced. . . . How indeed can we be conscious of a power to move our limbs, when we have no such power; but only that to move certain animal spirits, which, though they produce at last the motion of our limbs, yet operate in such a manner as is wholly beyond our comprehension?

(*Enquiry*, pp. 66–7)

The physiological mechanism is not relevant to the analysis of bodily experience. The experience of moving, or raising one's arm, of reaching for a pencil, of one's arm not as a thing but as the power to reach a thing, is another matter. But if the question is whether we experience power, how we acquire " the idea of power " – or to put the matter in another way, what " power " means – it is this experience, and not what objectively, physiologically, happens when we have this experience, which is the relevant consideration. Hume's argument is of exactly the same kind as his argument that taste and smell are *really* nowhere, which is to deny that one tastes a fig in one's mouth or smells a stink at a midden. The argument that we don't really see colours but only light of different wavelengths belongs to the same family; just as, according to this argument, we don't see what we think we see, so for Hume we don't do what we think we do when we move an arm.

Hume's discussion is dominated by the question of necessary connection, the grounds of inference from the past to the present and the logical problem of induction. Force, power, are treated simply as linguistic variants, and the animal nisus – the experience of effort and exertion of force, successful or unsuccessful – is dismissed as giving only a vulgar and inaccurate idea of power. But how in Hume's sense can an idea be accurate or inaccurate? In this particular case, he would have to say that the impression, i.e. the actual experience of effort, exertion, pushing, was inaccurate too. What he might demand is a more precise analysis of our actual experience, but he is not at all concerned to give that. His demand for more accuracy seems to be akin to the demand for more accuracy in an account of seeing a coloured surface. One can only describe some aspects of this, but one cannot say what a colour is, so far as direct experience of colour is concerned. Similarly, one cannot say what a push or a pull or pressure or exertion are in direct experience without using synonymous expressions: one can only describe various cases, which it is indeed important to do accurately. But Hume is demanding in the case of power or force, what he would not dream of demanding in the case of colour.

There is not of course a precise parallel. We open our eyes and there are the colours. But we only experience the resistance, pressure, weight, strength and force of things in opposition to the effort we have to make to shift and manipulate them in a variety of ways and in their various impacts upon us; but for our own doings and tasks as embodied beings, it goes without saying that we should have no such experience and these words would be meaningless (cf. Sartre, *L'Être et le Néant*, pp. 365–6). But this is a matter of direct embodied experience like our seeing colour, shape and extension, but not, as might be and often is wrongly supposed of these, the experience of a mere passive, contemplative being, but of a doer with hands and limbs. To do is to cause, but, I repeat, one isn't adding anything to the notion of doing by saying that.

One question which it is important and interesting to ask is why the story about volitions and movements of matter has been found so persuasive, for if it were not supported by some sort of experience it is unlikely that it would have survived and been widely accepted merely as the corollary of a metaphysical theory. What we must look for is the sort of experience which is readily transposed into the terms required by the theory. This sort of experience, of which it is said in traditional terms that the spirit is willing but the flesh is weak, is of the kind where there is indeed a conflict and *ipso facto* a certain duality, and which therefore lends itself to description in the dualistic terms of soul and body, will and body, or will and passions, where the passions are bodily passions. Here are some examples: one must get up to go to work, but the warmth, comfort and drowsiness are almost overwhelming; one wants to reach the summit of a mountain, but heat, thirst and fatigue make one falter – one is tempted to sink down and rest; one's anger is boiling up, but one tries to keep calm.

In these cases one is contending not – or not only – with an external situation but with what has happened to one bodily. Fatigue bears down, anger boils up, desire grips or impels, illness strikes, old age steals on. These things happen to one; one does not decide upon them or choose them, any more than one chooses to be born or where to be born. Hence they are so far like other given elements in one's situation – one must start from the given situation and act or react in one way or another. Since these happenings or states are bodily happenings or states, which one cannot help, it is natural to suppose that the spirit or will resists or succumbs, masters them or is defeated by them. But a moment's reflexion shows the fallacy. They are conscious; they are experiences; they are of the spirit as much as of the body. And on the other hand, the resistance, the attempt to overcome them is no less of the body than of the spirit: the will is a bodily will no less than when one is engaged in athletic combat. The unity of embodied experience is indissoluble. The mind–matter dualism applies plausibly to certain phases of it, but even in these the action or reaction of the will is bodily action. The will cannot act upon the body, for it is itself embodied. A doctrine which takes one's own body to be matter and nothing but matter must ignore the essential and original character of embodied experience. If the body as subject be rejected, the subject can only be a disembodied consciousness, not a seeing consciousness or a hearing consciousness and not a moving consciousness. The myth of the will is a myth of an unmoved mover, making non-motor movements.

The experience of moving and doing is inseparable from being a body. Hume's doctrine of perceptions does not deal with motion, other than perceived motion which strictly would be a succession of perceptions. In subsequent sensationalist doctrines, the experience of bodily movement was described as consisting of kinaesthetic sensations, and this, I think, takes the prize for idle verbalism.

Perceptions are essentially occurrences, events, happenings, as Hume indicates in saying that they are all of the nature of sensations like the pain of the cutting steel. That is to say that they are not doings. The mind or consciousness for Hume is often essentially passive, contemplative, and not active. Its propensities and dispositions are in effect happenings too. The association of ideas just happens. Such a passive consciousness could have no direct experience of power or causality, but only of succession, contiguity, repetition and constant conjunction. On the whole Hume has seeing in mind when he speaks of perceptions, but not looking. Looking is active: it is the way a doer with a task in hand sees. Hume thought he found in experience what his mechanical model of explanation and his physiological premises persuaded him he must find. He could only, however, think this in his study, not when he played backgammon or was merry with his friends.

For the contemplative consciousness not only is there no direct experience of power or force, there is no direct experience of possibility, impossibility or necessity. Even in its liveliest moments it is passive: " For after a frequent repetition, I find, that upon the appearance of one of the objects, the mind is determined by custom to consider its usual attendant, and to consider it in a stronger light upon account of its relation to the first object. 'Tis this impression, then, or determination, which affords me the idea of necessity." (*Treatise*, pp. 155–6.) Again: " We have established it as a principle, that as all ideas are derived from impressions, or some precedent *perceptions*, 'tis impossible we can have any idea of power or efficacy, unless some instances can be produced, wherein this power is perceiv'd to exert itself." (*Treatise*, p. 160.) Again: " We never have any impression, that contains any power or efficacy. We never therefore have any idea of power."

My examples of the direct experience of force or power in heaving or hoisting things would not count for Hume because doing is reduced to perceiving in a passive way and because a disembodied consciousness obviously cannot do anything. Nor can its objects have any function or use. The perception corresponding to what we call seeing a hammer is of a certain shape, size and colour and that is all. We cannot literally see a thing to knock in nails with, see its possibilities, see what we can do with it. We do not literally see what we can handle and grip: the visual is related to the tactual by association. That is to say, we can never see a *hammer*. A contemplative disembodied consciousness is not a doer and does not see as a doer. (It cannot, literally, see.)

Nothing for such a consciousness is possible, impossible or necessary. What happens, happens, and what does not, does not. Knowledge is knowledge of what happens. Since such a consciousness does not do anything, there is nothing it can or cannot do; but anything may happen or be joined to anything. There can be no necessary connection in the happenings contemplated by the passive consciousness. The necessity has to be just another happening that befalls it: " 'Tis this impression, then, or determination, which affords me the idea of necessity."

Let us then return to actual embodied experience, to pushes and pulls and dunts and doings, as well as to shapes and colours. It is not difficult to give examples of possibility, impossibility, and necessity. As in the case of power and force, they are not quasi-observed quasi-visually by a contemplative consciousness, but experienced in action. When I find I can or cannot do what I want to do by trying to do it, I experience possibility or impossibility. For example, a light bulb blows: I get up and raise my arm, trying to reach it, standing on tiptoe at full stretch; no, I cannot quite reach it, I cannot stretch far enough; I must get closer. I need the light for I want to go on writing. To replace the bulb I need something to stand on. I must get a chair. And that's it; that was what was needed.

To describe this as a series of happenings would be to describe it as a series of meaningless antics, if it were not that antics are antics only by contrast with conduct that makes sense, rational conduct. What I experience as happenings or events are only certain elements in the situation, for example, the light going out. But even that is not a mere event: I am writing and am suddenly deprived of light to write by; I need light and lack it. The extinction of the light is not a mere happening but a happening to me in my situation, writing in the light.

Only for an agent with desires and purposes, a *pour-soi* projecting a future, can there be any lack, anything missing, any negative experience. What I can and cannot do in pursuit of my purpose is what is possible or impossible. What I must do to achieve it is what is necessary. In order to understand practical necessity one must be a doer or agent. Like colour or force or deprivation, it can be described and talked about, but one must have had the experience to know what one is talking about.

The difficulty about necessity, possibility and impossibility in any but a logical context for the empiricist is that in the only terms acceptable to him these words can have no meaning. Whatever is not mere happenings, data, is knowledge, and the problem of knowledge is the problem of objective, scientific knowledge. In scientific experiment one waits to see what happens and then observes and notes the results. Though this peculiar experience becomes in empiricist doctrines the type of all experience and is read back into pre-scientific, pre-predicative experience, the model does not even apply to the case from which it is extracted. Objective experiments do not conduct themselves; nor do they happen, though they are designed to reveal what happens, under such and such conditions, if such and such be the case. If there were no embodied being who did not know but wanted to know what happens if . . . there would be no experiment. Only a subject can make an experiment and observe what happens. To observe, however, is not passively to contemplate, to be the recipient of data, but to know what to look for and to look for it. But in empiricist doctrines the very experience of the subject, the maker of experiments, is reduced to happenings, events and processes such as are observed in an experiment, and the only acceptable account of it is of the same kind as the account of what happens in the experiment.

The body is an object, so the only account of it can be a causal account. The subject, if any, is a pure mind. But for such a mind there could be no barriers, opportunities or prospects; doing nothing, it could not succeed or fail; experiencing no necessity, it could invent nothing; there could be nothing to circumvent, surmount, exploit or profit from. It could not know how; it could only know that.

Let us turn then to knowing *that*, to knowledge of matters of fact, of what is observably the case.

Whatever we observe is observed in a world of which it forms a part and in which we ourselves are, and in which we and it stand in a multiplicity of relationships to other things. Every "this" is "such-and-such": τόδε is always τοιόνδε. Without some of its relations, a thing cannot be conceived or described as being what it is – such and such a thing. Whatever is new and unfamiliar is so only in relation to what is familiar, the world as we already know it.

When Hume wants to illustrate the absence of causal necessity in what we actually observe, he takes the case of what we already conceive as billiard balls. These are spherical objects, hard, cold to the touch, heavy, smooth, which when struck roll silently over the green baize used in the game of billiards. Anyone who knows a billiard ball when he sees one, knows these defining characteristics. What do we mean when we say there is no necessity in the arrested motion of one and the imparted motion of another when the one impinges on the other? We can certainly imagine this not happening, even if we exclude from consideration all causes which might, unknown to us and contrary to our expectation, prevent it from happening. What we cannot logically do is to conceive billiard balls, used in the game of billiards as it is normally played, behaving otherwise than as they do. If they behave otherwise they are by definition not proper billiard balls (as prescribed in the book of rules) or it is not a proper table, or some other condition, explicit or implicit, of playing billiards is not fulfilled. To conceive them behaving otherwise is to conceive something else, for the concept of a billiard ball is the concept of a ball that behaves that way and billiards is possible only because it does: a ball is not just what is round, but what rolls and sets the other balls rolling. It must behave that way to be a billiard ball (though one can give the name of billiard ball to anything one pleases). We can predict that on impact with another billiard ball its motion will be arrested, as we can predict that if we look at the side of it which is not in view we shall find it smooth and curved like this side. In no sense, however, is the mind determined to pass from what it observes to what usually follows – it can pass to anything it pleases. From seeing the billiard ball rolling, we can pass to imagining it swerving round the other, rebounding, stopping dead, or rising vertically. But the logic of our present concept of a billiard ball requires that it behave as it does in fact behave. There is no reason[1] why a billiard ball or anything else should behave in a particular way or why it or anything else should exist, though the complex of conditions of its behaving as it does might be indefinitely extended. If its behaviour were completely irregular and unpredictable we could not conceive it as such-and-such at all. Nothing can be known of what offers no regularity and no pattern. Objects, says Hume, have no discoverable connection together. Unless they do they cannot be conceived or recognised.

Why do we believe that inductively established laws, causal relations, observed regularities, will hold good in future? What is the rational ground of prediction? Why do we believe that the future will be like the past, that laws which we have found to hold in the past will hold in the future? To answer this question, one must first ask what we mean by the future, how we conceive the future. What we mean by the future is not mere abstract futurity, but the future of the past and present. And the past and present as we conceive them are the way the world and everything in it has been and is, *so far as we know*. To conceive the future is to conceive the future of what there is, and we conceive what there is in terms of causal and many other relations. There are no other terms in which we can conceive the future. The sense in which many of our particular predictions and assumptions about the future may be unfulfilled is precisely the sense in which this has happened in the past: things, events and processes turned out not to be as we had supposed they were; we made mistakes. If the future is like the past there will be plenty of surprises for us; but we are familiar with surprises; we almost expect to be surprised. There can be no question of probability that the future will be like the past or present. If it is the future of the past or present it will be, for that is what we mean by the future. We can imagine what we please and dub this a possible future; but this is not the future of things and the world as we know them, which is *the* future.

[1] What sort of reason could that possibly be?

CHAPTER TWELVE

RUSSELL'S REDUCTION

The Analysis of Mind is carelessly written and it is often difficult to see how its arguments, drawn from the most disparate and diverse sources in scientific theory, may be connected. The doctrine which it attempts to expound is a form of " neutral monism ", of which Hume is the classic exemplar. In what follows, I have tried to concentrate on the essentials of the doctrine as they illustrate characteristically empiricist assumptions, ignoring the considerable part of the book which seems to me to be merely playful.

What Russell calls sensations, aspects, appearances or particulars correspond roughly to Hume's impressions. It is not clear how far they are deduced from physical or physiological theory and how far they are supposed to be given as such in experience. They are, however, the elements out of which minds on the one hand and physical objects on the other are somehow constructed or constituted. The difference lies in the relational structure, not in the stuff. Images, however, are peculiar to mind, and those particulars which are not sensations (if any) are peculiar to matter. But the elements as such or in themselves are neither mental nor physical, but neutral, occurrences.

Central to Russell's doctrine is the concept of a sensation which he takes over quite uncritically and which retains all its ambiguity. The doctrine is stated in Lecture V, ' Psychological and physical causal laws ':

A piece of matter as it is known empirically, is not a single existing thing, but a system of existing things. When several people simultaneously see the same table, they all see something different; therefore " the " table, which they are all supposed to see, must be either a hypothesis or a construction. " The " table is to be neutral as between different observers: it does not favour the aspect seen by one man at the expense of that seen by another. It was natural, though to my mind mistaken, to regard the "real" table as the common cause of all the appearances which the table presents (as we say) to different observers. But why should we suppose that there is some one common cause of all these appearances? As we have just seen, the notion of "cause" is not so reliable as to allow us to infer the existence of something that, by its very nature, can never be observed.

Instead of looking for an impartial source, we can secure neutrality by the equal representation of all parties. Instead of supposing that there is some unknown cause, the "real" table, behind the different sensations of those who are said to be looking at the table, we may take the whole set of these sensations (together possibly with certain other particulars) as actually being the table. That is to say, the table which is neutral as between different observers (actual and possible) is the set of all those particulars which would naturally be called "aspects" of the table from different points of view. (This is a first approximation, modified later.)

(Analysis, p. 97)

Russell, like Hume, is denying the "double existence", the perceptions and the unobserved cause of the perceptions, "something that, by its very nature, can never be observed". Russell is not just proposing another way of describing the ordinary experience of seeing a table, or at least does not intend just that. In Russell's terms two people can never *see* the same thing. Nor can one person *see* the same thing for two moments running unless he remains immobile. Nor can he have another look at what he saw before. Things seen are momentary occurrences, and an occurrence can never be repeated. Russell's reason for proposing this view is his assumption that people who would ordinarily be said to be looking at a table are having sensations, and that each sensation is an occurrence where each person is, and not where in the ordinary sense the table is. And this assumption is derived from the traditional sensationalist view in which the data or elements of experience are assimilated to bodily sensations which are where one's body, in the ordinary sense, is.

Though Russell rejects one form of the causal account of perception, his own view is inseparable from some such account, for one of the main reasons for holding that a patch of colour or aspect of a thing seen over there is really a sensation here, is that it is held to be the effect of a cerebro-neural process initiated by the stimulation of the retina. This cannot be, in itself or " really ", where we see it to be or as being – over there – for whereas the impingement of reflected light and the nervous impulse may be accounted for in physical and physiological terms, the final effect could not be accounted for in these terms if it were an occurrence at several yards or miles from the brain. And this is indeed Russell's view: a sensation occurs when a brain is part of the intervening medium.

This conflict between the doctrine of sensation and the way we see the alleged sensation may be avoided, as it is by Hume at times, by regarding the sensation as a mental event, an event in the mind, not in the world, and therefore as being in itself, or originally, or really, nowhere, for whatever is somewhere is spatially, physically, somewhere. But this of course raises the problem how we could ever know that there was a physical world, and that there is a physical world is the assumption of the whole causal theory. Bodily sensations are good candidates for the rôle of neutral stuff, for they are felt, and therefore mental or in the mind; but they are for example in the leg, and therefore bodily or in the body; so they are both mental and physical, or neither, neutral. But this does not get rid of the prior assumption of a physical world on which the whole theory depends, nor does it put the red of the sunset, as I see it, where my head is.

The view which regards the real table as the common cause of what several people would ordinarily be said to see from different angles is a view which Russell regards as natural, and no doubt it is. But it is not *the* natural view as this is displayed in ordinary language and conduct. The natural view is that the real table, or simply the table, is what we see in depth from one angle or another, not the cause of what we see. The table is the thing we write at, or have our dinner at, visible and tangible, and not the cause of what is visible and tangible.

It is not to be supposed for a moment that Russell does not know this; his very language makes this plain. But he never examines the experience of seeing a table or what people ordinarily mean by " table " and " seeing a table ". Instead he attacks the view [1] that the real table is an inferred entity, not actually seen or leant upon, not standing there in depth with a hither and a further side.

Russell continues (*Analysis*, p. 98): " It may be said: If there is no single existent which is the source of all these ' aspects ', how are they collected together? " From the natural standpoint, the question verges on absurdity. We walk round the table which stays where it is and one side disappears from view as another comes into view; we do not collect anything. If we suppose the question may be intelligibly asked, however, here is the answer:

The answer is simple: just as they would be if there were such a single existent. The supposed " real " table underlying its appearances is, in any case, not itself perceived, but inferred, and the question whether such-and-such a particular is an " aspect " of this table is only to be settled by the connection of the particular in question with the one or more particulars by which the table is defined. That is to say, even if we assume a " real " table, the particulars which are its aspects have to be collected together by their relations to each other, not to it, since it is merely inferred from them. We have only, therefore, to notice how they are collected together, and we can then keep the collection without assuming any " real " table as distinct from the collection. When different people see what they call the same table, they see things which are not exactly the same, owing to difference of point of view, but which are sufficiently alike to be described in the same words, so long as no great accuracy or minuteness is sought. These closely similar particulars are collected together by their similarity primarily and, more correctly, by the fact that they are related to each other approximately according to the laws of perspective and of reflection and diffraction of light. I suggest, as a first approximation, that these particulars, together with such

[1] This was his own view in *The Problems of Philosophy*.

correlated others as are unperceived, jointly *are* the table: and that a similar definition applies to all physical objects.

(*Analysis*, pp. 98-9)

It is worth remarking that this sort of view forms the basis for the formerly widespread intellectualist view of perception, which Russell at times adopts. According to this view, we interpret what we see, fill it out with images, theorise about it, and the result of all this is what we say we see or perceive. The model underlying this is of course the interpretation of evidence in solving a problem and seeking an explanation. Applying this model to perception, advocates of this view have to say that, of course, we do this unconsciously, thus putting the question beyond the reach of argument. Apart from that, however, it is difficult to understand how on this view there could be any such thing as veracious perception: the complaint about witnesses in law courts is precisely that they do not describe what they saw, but have drawn all sorts of conclusions from what they saw, taken dislikes to one party or another, which influences their account, etc. To see is precisely not to image or imagine. On the sort of view which Russell is propounding which takes the table to be a set of appearances in the flat, the squareness of the table has to be the result of interpretation, and depth perception of the table would be as it were a photogrammetrical reconstruction. I have called this view " intellectualist " since it seems to me evident that it assimilates perception to an intellectual operation (though one which, unlike such intellectual operations as solving logical problems, we are never aware of performing). But Russell's account of it (see, for example, *Analysis*, pp. 81, 112) merely asserts in effect that a perception is sensations, beliefs and images.

To return, however, to Russell's account of what a table is, it is clear enough that by aspects, appearances, particulars, Russell does not mean anything essentially different from sensations. But if by an aspect were meant as much of the table as is now visible over there, its location would be over there. And the same might be meant by an appearance of the table in one sense. But in that sense, neither an aspect nor an appearance would correspond to a sensation occurring where the observer was. It would simply be the now visible part of the table over there. In the other sense of "appearance" on which I have earlier dilated, the appearance of the table is the way the table looks to me or the way I see it, and it is a category mistake to attempt to assign a place to this either where I am or where the table is.

For Russell, however, as for Hume, appearances are occurrences and they are in the flat, not in depth; they are quasi-pictures. The squareness of the table cannot be seen except head-on. On this view, what people see when they look at a table-top is not the same shape from different angles and looking different from different angles, but different shapes " owing to difference in point to view ". This last phrase of course implies perception in depth, yet Russell supposes that what is seen is seen in the flat, a skew projection of the table-top from one angle or another. The table-top, therefore, is the set of skew projections of the table-top. As I have argued, it is only by supposing that these skew projections are like photographs with a surface that can be measured that they can be supposed to be anywhere or to have any measurable size. But looks of things are not photographs, nor are they anywhere. There is no question of describing different projections in the same words on account of their likeness " so long as no great accuracy or minuteness is sought ". The different looks from different angles are irremediably and necessarily different: if they weren't, the table would not be seen staying where it is as we move about it, and all these looks can perfectly well be described – foreshortening into a lozenge shape with two acute and two obtuse angles and so on. That is the way a square top looks from a certain angle in depth. If it did not look lozenge-shaped it would not be square and in depth. The square top is there; the lozenge shape is the way it looks *from* here, or *to* me here. But the lozenge shape is not here, nor is it anywhere. Russell's collection of skew projections would remain, as it were, a collection of flat pictures which would never coalesce; but only *as it were* a collection, for being at no distance they could not be seen. Nor could they be related to each other " according to the laws of perspective and of reflection and diffraction of light ", or collected together accordingly, for these laws presuppose planes and surfaces at different angles to each other in depth.

In the passages quoted, Russell has been concerned with sensations, appearances and observations, and is evidently intending, at least in part, to give an account of how what we call a thing is constituted in our perceptual experience. His next move, however, is apt to leave one bewildered.

> In order to eliminate the reference to our perceptions, which introduces an irrelevant psychological suggestion, I will take a different illustration, namely, stellar photography. . . . If we assume, as science normally does, the continuity of physical processes, we are forced to conclude that, at the place where the plate is, and at all places between it and a star which it photographs, *something* is happening which is specially connected with that star. . . . We can classify such happenings on either of two principles:
>
> (1) We can collect together all the happenings in one place, as is done by photography so far as light is concerned;
>
> (2) We can collect together all the happenings in different places, which are connected in the way that common sense regards as being due to their emanating from one object.
>
> (Analysis, p. 99)

To suppose that Russell is not concerned with sense-experience, as his reference to the elimination of irrelevant psychological suggestions might lead one to do, and to suppose that he is concerned only with physical processes, would be to miss the whole point of his argument. The point is to establish the identity, and neutrality as between mind and matter, of the elements or stuff which related in one way constitute mind and in another way constitute matter. The effect of the light on the photographic plate is regarded by Russell as essentially the same as the observed appearance of the star at the place where the plate is. But this is a preposterous view. What we see when we look at a star is not a photograph of the star where we are, nor is our seeing the star identifiable with any sort of picture or representation where our head is. The spot on the photographic plate is neither the star nor an appearance of the star.

Thus, to return to the stars, we can collect together either –
(1) All the appearances of different stars in a given place, or,
(2) All the appearances of a given star in different places.
But when I speak of " appearances ", I do so only for brevity;
I do not mean anything that must " appear " to somebody, but
only that happening, whatever it may be, which is connected, at
the place in question, with a given physical object. . . .

(Analysis, p. 100)

It is not necessary " for brevity " to speak of appearances at all, as
his words of explanation show. But it is necessary to his purpose to
speak of appearances, for he wants to identify what might be called
the appearances of the star to different observers, or different people
seeing the star, with happenings or occurrences where these people
are, like the happenings at the photographic plate. An appearance of
a thing is an effect or occurrence at another place.

According to the view that I am suggesting, a physical object
or piece of matter is the collection of all those correlated particulars
which would be regarded by common sense as its effects or appearances in different places. On the other hand, all the happenings
in a given place represent what common sense would regard as
the appearances of a number of different objects as viewed from
that place. All the happenings in one place may be regarded as
the view of the world from that place. I shall call the view of the
world from a given place a " perspective ". A photograph represents a perspective. On the other hand, if photographs of the stars
were taken in all points throughout space, and in all such photographs a certain star, say Sirius, were picked out whenever it
appeared, all the different appearances of Sirius, taken together,
would represent Sirius. For the understanding of the difference
between psychology and physics it is vital to understand these two
ways of classifying particulars, namely:
(1) According to the place where they occur;
(2) According to the system of correlated particulars in different
places to which they belong, such system being defined as a
physical object.

Given a system of particulars which is a physical object, I shall define that one of the systems which is in a given place (if any) as the " appearance of that object in that place ".

(*Analysis*, p. 101)

Russell seems actually to be foisting upon common sense the view than an appearance of an object is an effect or occurrence where one's head is. These alleged effects or occurrences are collectively the object. And all the happenings in one place (where one head in the ordinary sense is) are " what common sense would regard as the appearances of a number of different objects as viewed from that place ". But if the appearances are *in* that place they cannot be viewed *from* that place. Or is it appearances which are *in* and objects which are viewed *from*? On Russell's view objects cannot be viewed *from* anywhere, for they are simply collections of appearances *at* various places. This confusion of " from " and " to " with " at " or " in " is crucial in Russell's argument.

" All the happenings in one place may be regarded as the view of the world from that place." This amounts to saying, for example, that an occurrence where my head is may be regarded as my seeing the house across the street. But this experience cannot be located in my head; though I see with my eyes here, what I see is across the street. The word " perspective " is used to mean both " the view of the world from a given place " and " all the happenings in one place ".

A photograph, says Russell, "represents a perspective". In the ordinary way, this is true. But it is not true as Russell seems to mean it. What it represents in his sense is the occurrences at the photo-sensitive plate at the moment of exposure, and this is not the sense in which a photograph may be said to represent a perspective, e.g. a photograph of a landscape in perspective, from a point of view. In his sense, the occurrences in, or on, or at, the plate do not represent a perspective; they *are* a perspective. For Russell, a perspective, like " a view of the world from . . . ", is *in* one place. A picture of a landscape represents the landscape in perspective from a point of view. But the landscape one sees or the view of the landscape one has from where one is standing is not a picture and is not where one is standing.

Nor is Sirius or one's view of Sirius. But the photographs of Sirius are identified by Russell with the appearances of Sirius, and " all the different appearances of Sirius, taken together, would represent Sirius ". According to Russell's previous argument they would not *represent* Sirius, but *be* Sirius. But, it need hardly be said, a heap of photographs would not be Sirius. Russell continues:

> We can now begin to understand one of the fundamental differences between physics and psychology. Physics treats as a unit the whole system of appearances of a piece of matter, whereas psychology is interested in certain of these appearances themselves. Confining ourselves for the moment to the psychology of perceptions, we observe that perceptions are certain of the appearances of physical objects. From the point of view that we have been hitherto adopting, we might define them as the appearances of objects at places from which sense-organs and the suitable parts of the nervous system form part of the intervening medium. Just as a photographic plate receives a different impression of a cluster of stars when a telescope is part of the intervening medium, so a brain receives a different impression when an eye and an optic nerve are part of the intervening medium. An impression due to this sort of intervening medium is called a perception, and is interesting to psychology on its own account, not merely as one of the set of correlated particulars which is the physical object of which (as we say) we are having a perception.
>
> (*Analysis*, p. 104)

From this it would appear that perceptions occur at that place where, in the ordinary sense, the back of the head is, between which and the source of light lie the optic nerve and eyes as intervening medium. My seeing the house across the road is an occurrence behind my eyes. A perception is an impression which the brain receives. A set of such impressions – some *manquées*, since there are not brains everywhere – is the physical object, what we call the table or the house across the road.

There are certainly occurrences where heads are, such as those recorded by the E.E.G. But no such occurrences can be identified with the house across the road, with an appearance of a house across the road, or with our seeing a house across the road. Such occurrences are not part of perceptual experience, though they are found experimentally to be associated with it. The brain is itself a thing which has to be seen, examined and subjected to experiment for this fact to be established at all, just as one might see, examine and experiment with a stone from the house across the road. Russell forgets that the brain is itself a " physical object ", and therefore on his view of physical objects could not be part of an intervening medium between point A and point B, since it is the set of particulars or appearances everywhere but where in the ordinary sense it is. When he regards it as an intervening medium he takes it to be what is ordinarily meant by a thing or body in a certain position in relation to another thing. But that is not how he defines a physical object.

This inconsistent procedure is characteristic and far-reaching. The alleged position of any of his particulars or sensations is given by reference to what are ordinarily called things, spatially related to each other. If the reader did not understand what was meant by a brain or a table in this ordinary sense, which is not what Russell says a brain or a table is, he could not attempt to understand Russell's spatial references or his reconstruction of the world. But this understanding is founded on the actual experience of seeing things over there from here. There is no experience of seeing particulars where our heads are, no awareness of them. It is idle therefore to discuss residual problems such as how we would be led to postulate those particulars in the set which were not actual perceptions or sensations, or the manner of their collection into one system, or where and when one particular would end and another begin, spatially and temporally. It is of some interest, however, to examine Russell's view of space and time, which is very like Hume's.

CHAPTER THIRTEEN

RUSSELL'S VIEW OF
SPACE AND TIME

RUSSELL assumes spatial and temporal relations as these are commonly understood. Spatial relations are relations of things and events, and positions and spaces can only be specified by reference to these. For example, the window is beyond the table and the table is between the door and the window. But the place specified as " where the table is, between the door and the window " is not the place where the particulars of the set, which, according to Russell, is the table, are. It could not be identified or referred to if the table were what Russell says it is, for it is the spatial determination of the table (in the ordinary sense), where the table is, or between where the door is and where the window is, and nothing else. To assume otherwise is to suppose that space is not a relational order, but, as Kant expresses it, a self-subsistent non-entity, containing places which are where they are, irrespective of what there is, or is not, in them, or at them, and indeed whether there is, or is not, anything at all. To identify a place, as Russell does, by reference to a table or a brain, and then say in effect that the particulars of the set which is the table or the brain are not there, is not to identify any place at all. This is Russell's position : sensations are where your head is, but your head is not there.

A similar procedure is to be found in Russell's treatment of time in his chapter on memory:

> In investigating memory-beliefs, there are certain points which must be borne in mind. In the first place, everything constituting a memory-belief is happening *now*, not in that past time to which the belief is said to refer. It is not logically necessary to the existence of a memory-belief that the event remembered should

have occurred, or even that the past should have existed at all. There is no logical impossibility in the hypothesis that the world sprang into being five minutes ago, exactly as it then was, with a population that "remembered" a wholly unreal past. There is no logically necessary connection between events at different times; therefore nothing that is happening now or will happen in the future can disprove the hypothesis that the world began five minutes ago. Hence the occurrences which are *called* knowledge of the past are logically independent of the past; they are wholly analysable into present contents, which might, theoretically, be just what they are even if no past had existed.

(Analysis, pp. 159–60)

Russell's account of time and memory is based on the reduction of a memory *now* of an occurrence *then* to a complex occurrence *now*, just as his account of space and perception is based on the identification of the place where something is with the place from which it is seen, of *there* with *here*. But just as he takes for granted the distinction between the two places, so he continues to assume the distinction between the two times.

To say "It is not logically necessary to the existence of a memory-belief that the event remembered should have occurred" is to say no more than that we may be mistaken about what we saw or heard or did, that our memories may play us false. But to add "or even that the past should have existed at all" is not just to extend the previous statement but to make a different sort of statement. It is to say, not that we may be more or less mistaken about everything in the past, but that there may have been nothing we could remember well or ill, or fail to remember, that nothing at all may ever have happened, that there may have been no past. It is to apply to the entire past, to the totality of past events, to the world in the past, the sort of statement which can only significantly be made about particular events and things in the past, and this is to apply to past time the sort of statement which can only be made about things or events in times or at times, having time-determination.

"There was no rain in Edinburgh yesterday" is significant and may be true or false. But "There was no past" is self-contradictory, for the expressions "there was" and "there was not" essentially refer to the past and cannot be used to make true or false statements unless they do. The past is presupposed in the truth or falsity of such statements. "There was a past" is tautologous, and "there was not a past" self-contradictory.

The result of identifying consciousness and object is that anything anywhere and at any time, which we would ordinarily say we think of, or remember or imagine, is simply a component of a complex occurrence here and now. The various hypostases – perceptions, images, thoughts, memories – are all essentially present. Pastness therefore has to be a characteristic of a particular type of present complex, a date-stamp as it were. But the term "present" or "present event" is vacuous except in relation to past and future events. So is "now" except in relation to "then" (after or before, earlier or later). Past, present and future are correlative terms. It is perhaps most obvious that one cannot talk of the past or future without an implicit reference to the present: it is solely in relation to the present that anything can be said to be past. But it would be equally meaningless to talk of the present without any implicit reference to the past. The pastness of past events is their having occurred before present events, and the presence of present events is their occurring after past events. If pastness were merely a characteristic of a "belief-feeling", as Russell suggests, it would not be a present belief-feeling, since as such it would not have occurred after anything. It would not be really present if other events were not just as really past.

What we call one time, one moment or one period of time, is a time-determination of some event or events. The time of any event is the time it is in relation to the time-determinations of other events before and after. To insist with Kant that all beginnings are in time is to say they are after, or later than, something else. "There is no logically necessary connection between events at different times," says Russell. The sense in which there is a logically necessary connection is that all events are temporal events, before and after other events. The "first of all events" would not be an event, for it would have no time-determination, would not be at any time, there being no previous events and no previous times. The supposed time-determination " five minutes ago " in " the world sprang into existence five minutes ago " would not be a genuine time-determination, since it would not be after any other time-determination, there being no previous events.

To assume otherwise is to suppose that time is independent of the world, of what there is, of whether anything ever happens, and to suppose that even if there were nothing there would still be different times. This is, of course, the " self-subsistent non-entity " view of time, which derived whatever plausibility it had from regarding different times as themselves occurrences in times, before and after other times, just as the similar view of space regards different places or positions as being in different places or positions in space. On any other view, however, " an event five minutes ago " implies " something else before that ".

On Russell's " logically possible " hypothesis, not only the word " remember " would require the quotation marks he gives it, but also " past " and " present ". What we called the past would not be really past, but neither would what we called the present be really present. For we would not know the date. The present time is, for example, twenty years after the Second World War; Russell is an old man; some people are old, some young; some industries are developing, some in decay. The whole present state of affairs is understood in terms of the past and cannot be spoken about without implicit reference to it. It is meaningless to talk of the present apart from what there is now, the present state of affairs, and what there is now includes old and young, new and old, activities in progress, processes which were begun before now, and so on. To omit the numerous quotation marks which the hypothesis would require is to display the contradiction in saying there is a present but there was no past. Innumerable " true " propositions, particular and general, would be untrue, and it is these which define what we take to be the present. " We " should be " living " under a complete " illusion " if we " ' remembered ' a wholly unreal past ". The " present " would not be the present.

The error in the hypothesis arises from what one may call the naturalistic or psychologistic fallacy. The essence of this fallacy is the attempt to reduce subjectivity to objectivity, consciousness to object, to reduce seeing, knowing, believing, feeling, desiring, etc., to certain kinds of complex occurrences. The effect in the case of knowing or remembering in particular is paradoxically a subjectivist theory of knowledge and truth, the occurrences here and now constituting knowing or remembering, being logically independent of whatever else is the case.

CHAPTER FOURTEEN

THE NATURALISTIC FALLACY

I⊤ should be said at the outset that victims of the psychologistic fallacy generally evade its consequences at the cost of radical inconsistency. In what follows I shall try both to expose the fallacy and to show how it is evaded.

The hypostatised image plays an essential part in Russell's account of mind. He takes it to be a mental occurrence, a sort of picture, which we can contemplate and whose relation to anything else – what, in the ordinary sense, it would be said to be *of* – is inferential. Strictly, the observing of it would have to be another mental occurrence, but though Russell discusses this point in his chapter on introspection, he never resolves it. An image for Russell as for Hume is a copy of a sensation, but since to remember a sensation is to have an image and there is no *other* way of remembering a sensation, this can never be known, for each is simply a present occurrence. And so are the present beliefs and belief-feelings which are supposed to establish the relation of the one to the other.

> The reference of thoughts to objects is not, I believe, the simple direct essential thing that Brentano and Meinong represent it as being. It seems to me to be derivative, and to consist largely in *beliefs*: beliefs that what constitutes the thought is connected with various other elements which together make up the object. You have, say, an image of St Paul's, or merely the word " St Paul's " in your head. You believe, however vaguely and dimly, that this is connected with what you would see if you went to St Paul's, or what you would feel if you touched its walls: it is further connected with what other people see and feel, with services and the Dean and Chapter and Sir Christopher Wren. These things are not mere thoughts of yours, but your thoughts stand in a relation

to them of which you are more or less aware. The awareness of this relation is a further thought, and constitutes your feeling that the original thought had an " object ". But in pure imagination you can get very similar thoughts without these accompanying beliefs; and in this case your thoughts do not have objects or seem to have them. Thus in such instances you have content without objects.

(Analysis, p. 18)

Though these remarks are indeed preliminary, as Russell says, there is nothing in them which seriously misrepresents Russell's position, and if they are obscure nothing he says later really makes them less so. It is intended to be an account of what happens when one images or imagines St Paul's. According to Russell's account, we have an image which we believe is connected with St Paul's or what we should see if we went to St Paul's. But it may be asked, if we think of what we should see if we went to St Paul's what is this but to image St Paul's? The only case which would at all fit Russell's description is the case where we imagine something which we cannot quite place, when we have to try to place what we are imagining – a certain domed building, say. For Russell, however, our image is a picture, of which the connection with St Paul's has to be established by the feeling or belief that they are related. To have an image of St Paul's there must be the image, the thought of St Paul's, and the belief, if not other "thoughts" as well. Now there is no doubt that Russell means by " St Paul's " that very cathedral in the City. When one images St Paul's, however, the meaning is not something apart from the image. To image St Paul's is to mean that very cathedral. When one imagines St Paul's, it is ipso facto St Paul's one is imagining. To image is one mode of intending or meaning an object. St Paul's is the intended or meant object, even if meanwhile some catastrophe has befallen it and it is no more.

For Russell, however, images are entities, and are not essentially of anything. As for others who hold this view, his problem is to distinguish them from sensations either by their inherent characteristics or by their causal antecedents, and the latter he regards as the only reliable way (*Analysis*, p. 149). These causal antecedents are brain processes, initiated in the case of sensations at the external sense organs and in the case of images within the brain. This is not how in fact we do distinguish them. But what he says of the brain processes with which they are respectively associated is no doubt true. The obvious reason for holding it to be true, however, is the distinction we do make between seeing something and imagining something. When we see something it is there before our eyes, but when we imagine something it is usually not, and if it is, it is difficult to imagine and not see it. If we did not make this distinction independently of any causal theory about seeing and imaging, we could not make the sort of distinction Russell proposes, for we would not know whether we were seeing or imagining the evidence for brain processes.

Russell's account of memory is closely related to his view of images. The image is a present occurrence and the pastness of what is remembered is reduced to a present belief-feeling. What this belief-feeling is about is a present image. The belief " may be expressed in the words ' this existed ' ". It is simply a " specific kind " of present belief-feeling – " the reference to the past lies in the belief-feeling, not in the content believed " (*Analysis*, p. 186). " In the simplest kind of memory we are not aware of the difference between an image and the sensation which it copies, which may be called its ' prototype '. When the image is before us, we judge rather ' this occurred '. The image is not distinguished from the object which existed in the past: the word ' this ' covers both, and enables us to have a memory-belief which does not introduce the complicated notion ' something like this '."

It is true that the image is not distinguished as an entity from what it is of, for it is not before us and is not an entity or quasi-object. When we now imagine something past, there is only one object – something past. But Russell wants to suggest that the unsophisticated or simple person, of whom he makes great play in this chapter, does not distinguish between something past and something present. When we recall something in imagination it is that very thing or situation we mean. If we say " this occurred " we mean what did occur and there is no confusion of this with whatever is occurring now. Russell's story about the imprecision of unsophisticated people is a tall one. He wants to suggest that they fail to distinguish the picture before them from the past event which it represents. This would not be true even if an image were a picture: as if when someone said, " That's the battle of Lepanto on the wall ", he actually thought there was a battle in progress on the wall.

The problem is how to get the references to the past into an analysis of memory which leaves no room for anything but present occurrences. Russell's procedure is simply to assert that the present belief-feeling refers to the present image, and the time-determination " past " lies in the nature of the feeling, not in the image. But in what sense can the time-determination " past " lie in a present feeling any more than in a present image? The only time-determination which could " lie in " either would be " present ". The nature of the belief-feeling, we are told " is that called ' remembering ' or (better) ' recollecting '. It is only subsequent reflexion upon this reference to the past that makes us realise the distinction between the image and event recollected. When we have made this distinction, we can say that the image ' means ' the past event." If the reference to the past were in the belief – "a specific feeling or sensation or complex of sensations" – incomprehensible though this might be, we should be remembering. But that won't do, for what we should be " remembering " would still be a present image. So we have by reflection to realise the distinction between the image and the event recollected.

But how on earth on Russell's theory do we ever make this distinction? It is hard to resist the conclusion that Russell simply realised that the past event had to be got in somehow if " memory " was to be memory at all, and made it materialise by " subsequent reflexion ". This reflexion would of course be distinct from the happenings and occurrences to which mental life would be otherwise reducible, and to which he set out to show it would be entirely reducible. The " past " event, however, need not be a past event, for as we have seen, on Russell's view, it is logically possible that there was no past, and therefore that there is no memory, but only " memory " of the past.

Russell's doctrine is based upon physical and psychological theory, of which he takes various aspects as premises of his analysis of what there is and of his reduction of perceiving, believing, knowing, etc., to occurrences. The spatial and temporal orders are assumed in the premises, but the reduction of mental life to present occurrences then suggests the possibility that there was no past. But if there were no past, the premises, physical and psychological, would be false. The hypothesis could only be advanced if the analysis of all there is, including knowledge, into occurrences were true, but the truth of the hypothesis would falsify the analysis. It is true that the logical structure of Russell's doctrine is very difficult to discern, but it is evident that his crucial arguments are taken from physics and to a somewhat less extent from psychology. The essence of the naturalistic fallacy is the attempt to explain experience in terms of natural sciences whose only evidence lies in experience. Russell's scientistic assumption is that whatever may be known about " mind " is to be scientifically, empirically known, and this means by external or " internal " observation.

Before I deal with behaviourism and introspectionism I would like to deal with an older example of the psychologistic fallacy, now universally abandoned – the attempt to reduce the principle of contradiction and the other " laws of thought " to facts of human psychology, to beliefs or convictions, which, though peculiarly forceful, might nevertheless have been otherwise. This amounts to saying that it is logically possible that the principle of contradiction should not be true, that its denial is not self-contradictory. But if it were not true, this statement itself could not be true or false.

To understand other cases of the fallacy, it is not enough to rest content with the distinction between on the one hand analytic, logical or necessary truths, and on the other hand synthetic, factual and contingent truths. We must examine the premises which led to the attempt to reduce logical truth to contingent truth, logic to psychology, for these assumptions are essentially the same as those which lead to the attempt to reduce the past to present "memories", things seen to present perceptions, things imaged to present images and belief-feelings, facts known to the knowing of " facts ", and so on. The assumption which is common to doctrines attempting to reduce logical truth to psychological fact is that mental life is reducible to causally connected events, occurrences, processes, and states, psychological facts which are empirically observed by an " inner perception " or introspection. This assumption no doubt dates back to Locke's account of the ideas of reflexion which are acquired by the mind's attention to its own activity about its ideas of sensation. On such a view, introspection is no less a source of empirical knowledge than external observation. What is observed is events and processes which may be subsumed under various laws of succession and association, by the formulation of hypotheses and their experimental verification, as in physics. The process of perceiving and thinking, the state of knowing, may be thus described and the laws which govern the occurrences constituting these activities may be formulated.

Notoriously, things did not quite work out that way, but this could be put down to the peculiar difficulties of the subject matter, as could differences in the procedures of biology and physiology, say, as compared with physics. In principle, the mind was a domain of empirical investigation no less than the physical world. If knowledge of the mind were possible at all it must be empirical knowledge, knowledge of observed facts and verified hypotheses. And the processes which constitute knowing must be known, if at all, in this way. Now if thought and knowledge are reducible to mental processes and states, the "laws of thought" must be laws governing mental processes, though of a very general and fundamental character, and the fact that mental processes do not always appear to conform to these laws – logical errors are very common – may be ascribed to countervailing causes, as may, for example, that fact that the compass needle does not always point north. (Why one process or succession of occurrences should be considered *erroneous* as compared with another remains a mystery, for what is simply is, and Hume's theory of knowledge is itself open to this very objection.) Thus the laws of thought like the laws of association would be empirically established laws governing mental phenomena. What is true would be what we believe with conviction, and of the laws of thought we are completely convinced. They are the most general, most indispensable of laws, but they simply happen to be as they are. Their necessity remains a contingent, psychological necessity.

If such a doctrine merely asserted that it was psychologically possible to believe a logical impossibility, to believe that a logical contradiction was true, it would not be open to any radical objection. To believe that a logical contradiction is true is to fail to realise that it is a logical contradiction; logical contradictions are not all self-evident, but often very difficult to detect. But what is asserted is not just this commonplace, but that we could recognise a contradiction and believe it to be true. Being physically as we are, we cannot fly like birds. Being mentally as we are, we cannot recognise a contradiction and believe it to be true: it is a psychological impossibility. This impossibility is contingent, *de facto*, like our inability to fly. But if this were so, how could we know it was contingent or suppose that it could be otherwise? It would be psychologically impossible. But what then could " contingent " mean but " not logically necessary "? And this would simply re-establish the distinction which the theory set out to abolish. If we believed logical contradictions to be true, e.g. that " p is true and p is false " is true, we should simply be in error, making a logical blunder, failing somehow to recognise the meaning of " true " and " false ", of " is " and "is not", of assertion and denial. These meanings are assumed in all empirical investigation.

The psychologistic view is not only untenable as regards logic and knowledge of logical truths, it is equally untenable as regards empirical knowledge, perception, memory, thought, feeling, desire, etc. On the psychologistic theory we could be said to know or apprehend a matter of fact, or the truth of the proposition expressing it, only when a certain conjunction of mental phenomena, itself a state of affairs or matter of fact, came to pass. How then would one determine the truth of the proposition " I know that this typewriter is on the table "? To know that we knew the typewriter was on the table, we should have to know that the typewriter was on the table but also we should have to know the mental matter of fact constituting our knowing this. But to know that we knew these two matters of fact, we should have to know these matters of fact plus the higher order mental matters of fact constituting our knowing them. And so on, *ad infinitum*. Similarly to know that " I see a typewriter " was true, we should have to know that there was a typewriter in a certain place and that the mental occurrences constituting seeing were actually occurring, and that the relation between these occurrences was of the appropriate kind.

A further difficulty is the " systematic elusiveness " of the introspective observation. If empirical observation of the introspective kind were possible at all, it would involve all or most of the " activities " which it investigates, but these would not be what was investigated or observed; it would not be observing its own activity, the activity of introspection. It is hard to say what the mind would be observing, but its procedure would be objective, scientific and empirical only at the cost of failing to do what it sets out to do – to observe its own activities.

For empiricism there are two sorts of knowledge – knowledge of logical truths and knowledge of matters of fact. But if the mind were as some empiricist doctrines have held it to be, neither kind of knowledge would be possible. For knowledge itself would be entirely reducible to mental states, events and processes – matters of observable fact – and knowledge of any matter of fact would therefore itself be reducible to a matter of fact. The state constituting knowledge, being a matter of fact, could have only a *de facto* relation to any state of affairs in the world. The relation of knowing to what was known would be external and contingent. The state constituting " knowing that X is A " would be logically compatible both with " X is A " and " X is not A ", since the mental state would be only contingently related to the other state of affairs. If knowing were a mental state of affairs it would not necessarily be untrue to say " I know that X is A " if X were not in fact A. If, however, one defines the relation of knowing to known in such a way that this would be contradictory, nevertheless, according to the introspectionist doctrine, one would have to know both what the external state of affairs was and what the mental state of affairs was in order to determine whether the relationship between them constituted a case of knowledge. But how could one know that one knew what the external state of affairs or the internal state of affairs were? Each of these would be constituted by a relation between two states of affairs and so on.

If it is asserted that no introspectionist ever actually held such a doctrine, my reply is that if introspection is held to be empirical observation (as it commonly was) there is no escape from the above absurdities. It is because introspectionists commonly take another kind of knowledge, which they will not recognise as knowledge, for granted that what they say is often plausible.[1] And it is true that the word " introspection " has been used in many ways. A subject describing what he sees in an experiment in perception, for example, would be described by some psychologists as giving an introspective report, a usage which identifies introspection with extraspection. What I am concerned to attack is the view that there is any sort of empirical observation apart from the commonly recognised kind – external perception of things and events in the world.

People say, for example, " I know the height of the Eiffel Tower ", or "I am listening to the radio " or " I see a man over there " or " I remember meeting Tom last week ". These verbs in the first person singular are among the commonest in the English language. Prima facie, everyone understands such expressions, knows what they mean, and assumes that they can be true or false. This common under-standing is the starting-point of any analysis, philosophical or psycho-logical, of mind. Since people do not suppose that any introspective observation is required to verify them, since they are unaware oe making any such observation when they make such assertions, therf would seem to be no ground for holding that they do. For everyone admits that the basis for such assertions as " There is a fly in my tea " is observation, but statements beginning " I know . . . " or " I see . . . " or " I hear . . . " are just as common and if they were founded on introspective observation how could people fail to be aware of this?

Part of the inspiration of behaviourism was the need to reject intro-spection as a source of empirical knowledge. For the consistent behaviourist – *relatively* consistent – " seeing ", " knowing ", " listen-ing to ", " thinking ", " being in pain ", etc., all essentially refer to observable public happenings, just as a dog's hunger *is* its salivation, tail-wagging, etc. Behaviourism has this signal virtue that it is not concerned with alleged ghostly happenings in a non-spatial place called the mind, but with visible, observable happenings. But the re-duction of mental life to externally observable states, events, and processes leads to a difficulty no less acute than its reduction to internally observable states, events and processes. A strict behaviourist must

[1] See below, pp. 132 f.

feign anaesthesia, or possibly accept solipsism. It is commonly supposed that people can feel pain, say a pain in the leg, and that groans and the screwing up of the face and so on are the expression or symptoms of the pain, but not the pain itself. And the purpose and virtue of anaesthetics are held to be the stopping of the pain itself. But a strict behaviourist would be obliged to hold that their purpose is to change the patient's behaviour, to stop him screwing up his face and groaning and talking about the pain in his leg. But everyone maintains that he knows what pain is, what " pain " means, and it certainly is not publicly observable antics.

Again, a behaviourist must observe the behaviour of the so-called subject, the dog or the baby, but it would seem that without external observation of his own behaviour he cannot be said to know that he has observed the dog or the baby. He cannot know that he sees the dog unless he sees himself seeing. And if it be supposed that he might think over the experiments of the day alone in his armchair in the evening or wonder whether to go to the cinema, the only evidence of this would be incipient vocal movements in the throat, which he does not observe and could not know he was observing if he did. There is no evidence acceptable to him as a behaviourist that he is thinking at all and no evidence that he has mental images or images anything.

Again, it will be said this is a caricature. No behaviourist denies conscious experience, and it is precisely because it is not empirically observable that he decides for reasons of method to ignore it. This is perhaps too kind to behaviourists; it is unwise to take the plea of philosophical asepsis at its face value. I shall argue, however, that the behaviourist does not ignore conscious experience but takes it entirely for granted.

Introspectionism and behaviourism have in common the assumption that the only knowledge of mind as of matter is empirical knowledge, knowledge of fact, and such knowledge is founded on observation of states, events and processes. The model of observation is what everyone means by observation – looking and seeing what happens – which is no less indispensable for the verification of an elaborate scientific hypothesis than for the common purposes of every day. But if this model applied to our supposed knowledge of the mind, if the evidence for the truth or falsity of statements beginning " I see . . . ", " I am wondering whether . . . ", " I am uneasy about . . . " were obtained by observation in anything like this sense, " I " would not refer to the speaker any more than " effervescent liquid in the test-tube " refers to the chemist. But no one seriously supposes that he has to make observations on which to base assertions that he sees, is wondering whether, is uneasy about, is thinking that, or knows that, or remembers that. And if to know is to know by empirical observation, he does not and cannot know that he sees, hears, etc.

But the common conviction is that such statements can be true or false and that there must be a sense in which we can know whether they are true or false. These expressions plainly refer not simply to events and happenings in the world but to our experience of them and the various ways in which we experience them. This experience is made explicit in reflexion or self-awareness; for example, the experience of being a body here seeing something over there. When we simply describe what we see, we are not describing this experience, but what is reflexively described is implicit in our seeing and in the visibility of what is seen. If reflexion or self-awareness were not completely commonplace in the way which I have tried to elaborate earlier, some of the commonest and most familiar expressions of the language would be hard to understand – " I see . . . ", " I've got it! " (said on solving a problem), " I remember . . . ", " I seem to remember . . . ". But everyone understands them to all appearances as I understand them, and I understand them because I know what it is to see, to think, to wonder, to be puzzled, to have a flash of illumination, to remember, etc. Such statements of experience are not incorrigible, nor, lying apart, are they always true, for the experience of seeing, for example, is inseparable from something seen, and we may mistake an after-image for a patch on the wall. (Whether we say we see an after-image, however, or just have an after-image, is a matter of little moment – its peculiarities are easily enough discerned by reflexion. So indeed are the peculiarities of the empiricist philosopher's hobby-horse – hallucinations – according to those who have had them.)

Our experience as embodied beings is taken for granted in all intelligible observation-statements about the world. Such statements do not refer to it, but it is solely by virtue of it that they refer to any-thing at all. Objectivity is the correlate of subjectivity. The attempt to reduce the one to the other merely leads to confusion, for it deprives words of their meaning and their meaning is neither more nor less than what we mean by them. The explication and analysis of linguistic meaning is useless unless it is an analysis of what we do mean by the expressions we use. The correctness of such an analysis is not a matter of inductive observation of the circumstances in which the expressions in question occur, as it might seem to be if the injunction " look for the use " were to be followed. The only question is: would I say that in such and such a case? Is that what I mean by . . .? And this is known by reflexion, not by any sort of empirical observation. For language, the power of speech and expression, is like all my skills embodied in me. I am in possession of it. Nobody who wasn't would have the remotest idea what J. L. Austin, for example, was talking about.

Such plausibility as the introspectionist and behaviourist doctrines have depends on the common understanding of what expressions referring to experience mean, the reflexive understanding of what it is to see, hear, be hungry, be depressed, think, wonder, desire, etc. In order to say what their topic is – hunger, anger, fear, etc. – they have to use the words whose meaning everyone knows, and it is mere obscurantism to put them in quotation marks. It is an illusion to suppose that these words are merely used by way of introduction in their ordinary meanings, later to be abandoned. Behaviourism remains secretly dependent throughout on such ordinary meanings. The physiological symptoms and visible manifestations of hunger and anger, for example, as the behaviourist describes them could only be described and grouped as related manifestations by one who already knew what hunger and anger were like, what it was to be angry and to be hungry, and to be embodied. When anger is thereafter redefined as an observable type of antic, the secretion of adrenalin, increase in blood sugar, etc., this is a mere assertion that the meaning of " anger " is not what we normally mean by " anger ". But the entire discourse depends for its intelligibility upon our already knowing what anger is by having been angry.

The conclusive argument similarly against Russell's analysis in *The Analysis of Mind* of what " Napoleon " means or what we mean by " Napoleon ", is that we mean what we mean and we do not mean what Russell says we mean, either by " Napoleon " or by " table ". This is no low, vulgar jibe, though in Hume's sense of " vulgar " I mean to be vulgar. For either we do not mean what Russell says we mean by " Napoleon " or we do not mean what Russell means by " what we mean ". From a description of Napoleon in Russell's terms (sets of series and series of sets of sensations, etc.) it would be utterly impossible to know who or what was being described, much less to learn anything of interest about him or it. Compared with this vulgar objection, the criticism of Russell's doctrine is mere trifling, though it would seem to be an equally conclusive objection to his theory that we are never aware of the alleged " ultimate brief existents that go to make up the collections we call things or persons " and which would be spoken of " by means of some elaborate phrase, such as ' the visual sensation which occupied the centre of my field of vision on January 1, 1919 '." In this phrase of Russell's everything is intelligible except the word " sensation ", for the field of vision is simply the field of seeing – what one has within sight with one's head in one position – but one cannot ask of the sensation what distance it was at, one can only ask that of things and events in the world that one sees in depth. The elaborate phrase does not refer to anything such as one ever experiences.

The short answer to the question " How do you know you see, hear, think, are pleased, etc.? " is " By seeing, etc. ", or " Because I *do* see, etc. " People tend to be baffled and bewildered by the question, and if they produce this answer they tend to feel that it is not really an answer at all. (Russell takes this view in his discussion of an article by Knight Dunlap, the American psychologist, who gives what is essentially this answer.) (*Analysis*, pp. 114–15.) I think it is essentially the correct answer, and I think it is also understandable why it is felt not to be an answer. In all their enquiries and investigations and projects and actions, people take themselves for granted; being an embodied consciousness is the *a priori* condition of projects, actions, and investigations. Reflexion or self-awareness merely makes explicit what is implicit, in the sense that we take it for granted. If reflexion were not commonplace, we could not use or understand the countless ordinary words which refer to and describe, not only what is the case in the world, but our experience of it, and words such as " here " and " now " which have no meaning apart from our experience of embodied being, being a body. But the meaning of all these words is taken for granted in expositions of doctrines of mind and body which, if true, would make our ordinary understanding of them impossible.

Russell's is such an account. His account of experience does not start from experience, but from physics, and what it boils down to is the assertion that what we mean by the ordinary words describing experience is not what they really mean but just what we imagine or suppose they mean. There is no better example, though there are many others, than Russell's account of a table.

If philosophy is to give an account of experience, it must be concerned with the actual experience we do have and not with hypothetical or possible " experiences " we do not have, nor derive from physical and other theories, the evidence for which is acquired by the experience we do have, an account of experience as it must be, in Russell's naïve phrase, " if physics is true ".

CHAPTER FIFTEEN

WHY SENSE-DATA?

WHEN Hume cites houses, trees and mountains as examples of impressions, or uses the words "object" and "impression" indifferently, or says that the vulgar take their perceptions to be their only objects, one may occasionally wonder whether the doctrine of impressions and ideas is anything more than a way of talking. But it is plain that Hume believes that impressions and ideas are what there really is, that they are known to us by consciousness, as he says, such as they really are, and that they are as they appear, whatever we take them to be.

The authors of sense-datum doctrines in the past seventy years have mostly supposed like Hume that they were making assertions about perceptual experience and the objects of perceptual experience, and not merely proposing another way of talking about them. Some, however, and notably A. J. Ayer in *The Foundations of Empirical Knowledge*, have maintained that such doctrines, properly understood and revised accordingly, are no more than proposals to adopt a linguistic expedient, to talk in a certain way, and to use a less ambiguous language, for philosophical purposes. And Ayer himself intends to do no more. It is my purpose to show that, on the contrary, Ayer's position can be assimilated to Hume's, by virtue of an unargued Humean premise which governs the whole course of his discussion.

If we accept this recommendation [to use a sense-datum language] it will not be because our ordinary language is defective, in the sense that it does not furnish us with the means of describing all the facts, or in the sense that it obliges us to misdescribe some of them; but simply because it is not so good an instrument as the sense-datum language for our special purposes. For since in philosophising about perception our main object is to analyse the relationship of our sense-experiences to the propositions we put forward concerning material things, it is useful for us to have a terminology that enables us to refer to the contents of our experiences independently of the material things that they are taken to present. And this the sense-datum language provides.

(Foundations, p. 26)

The premise that sense-experiences may be considered independently of things in the world is not stated as such, but simply taken for granted in Ayer's statement of the object of philosophising about perception. The proposed terminology " enables us only to refer to familiar facts in a clearer and more convenient way ". It is by virtue of his Humean premise that Ayer believes we can so refer to familiar facts. Thus we may consider the sense-experience or perception or content independently of the cat on the mat or the house across the road or the mist in the valley, which they are taken to present. That is to say, the content or sense-experience would not be the cat or the house or the mist, or something that we took for a cat or a house or mist, but something else. What else? What could it be but the look of the cat, the look of the house or the look of the mist? Whether the cat or the house or the mist were or were not what we took them to be, they would certainly look as they looked – and also look *like* what they looked *like*.[1] Contents or perceptions or sense-data can only be the hypostatised looks of things. To say, as Ayer does, that sense-data are indubitable or " veridical " and sense-datum statements incorrigible, amounts at best to no more than this: that however mistaken we may be about what things are, they do look the way they look. Looks are unmistakable, for the way things look is the way we actually see them.

But looks are not independent of things or of us embodied beings who see, from where we are, the things where they are; nor can they be intelligibly spoken of as if they were. In the sense-datum doctrine, however, as in the doctrines from which it descends, looks are hypostatised and become the entities which we are said to sense or to be aware of. The premise is simply assumed and finds expression quite casually in arguments based upon it.

[1] See below, pp. 146-7.

In the following passage, Ayer is citing a classic argument, which he indeed proceeds to criticise, but in a way, as we shall see, which strikingly reveals the Humean premise.

> Thus, if I gradually approach an object from a distance I may begin by having a series of perceptions which are delusive in the sense that the object appears to be smaller than it really is.[1] Let us assume that this series terminates in a veridical perception. Then the difference in quality between this perception and its immediate predecessor will be of the same order as the difference between any two delusive perceptions that are next to one another in the series . . . the relation between a veridical perception and the delusive perception that comes next to it in the series is the same as that which obtains between neighbouring delusive perceptions, both with respect to the difference in quality and with respect to the change in the conditions; and these are differences of degree and not of kind. But this, it is argued, is not what we should expect if the veridical perception were a perception of an object of a different sort, a material thing as opposed to a sense-datum. . . . And from this it would follow, if it was acknowledged that the delusive perceptions were perceptions of sense-data, that what we directly experienced was always a sense-datum and never a material thing.
>
> (Foundations, pp. 8–9)

Ayer's criticism of this argument is that it does not prove what it is meant to prove, viz., that we are always, or ever, mistaken in believing that the objects we immediately perceive are material things, since we cannot prove they are not. He accepts, however, the argument that if we take all our " perceptions " to be " veridical " and at the same time believe that what we are seeing is a material thing which remains unchanged, we land in a contradiction. The contradiction can then be removed by simply not assuming that the thing remains the same:

> I have shown that the ground on which it is maintained that

---

[1] If the " object " were a man, this would naturally mean that he appeared to be a very small man. But this does not seem to be what Ayer means.

there are at any rate some occasions on which we perceive sense-data which are not parts of any material things [1] is that some perceptions are delusive; and the ground on which it is maintained that some of our perceptions must be delusive is that if we take them all to be veridical we shall involve ourselves in contradictions, since we shall have to attribute to material things such mutually incompatible properties as being at the same time both green and yellow, or both elliptical and round. But here it may be objected that these contradictions cannot, in fact, be derived from the nature of our perceptions alone. If from one standpoint I see what appears to be a round coin and then, subsequently, from another standpoint, see it as elliptical, there is no contradiction involved in my supposing that in each case I am seeing the coin as it really is. The supposition becomes self-contradictory only when it is combined with the assumption that the real shape of the coin has remained the same.

(Foundations, p. 14)

Since this latter assumption, Ayer continues, is not logically necessary, it must be validated on empirical grounds. And on these grounds it may be denied, he maintains, without fear of refutation, by anyone who chooses to do so.

One may imagine him saying, for example, that the fact that the shape of the penny still appears the same when the observer returns to his original point of view does not prove that its real shape has been unchanged; for it might be the case that the shape that it originally appeared to have was in reality altered and then regained. . . . How then is one who holds this position to be refuted? The answer is that so long as we persist in regarding the issue as one concerning a matter of fact it is impossible for us to refute him. We cannot refute him, because, as far as the facts are concerned, there is really no dispute between us. It has been assumed that he agrees with us about the nature of the sensible appearances; and no evidence of any other kind is or can be

---

[1] Looks, of course, are not parts of material things: parts of things are smaller things or *bits* of things.

available. In what then does our disagreement consist? It consists in the fact that he refuses to describe the phenomena in the way in which we describe them. When we say that the real shape of the coin is unchanging, he prefers to say that its shape is really undergoing some cyclical process of change.

(Foundations, pp. 17–18)

Ayer and his imaginary interlocutor agree about the nature of sensible appearances: they agree that these appearances are what is given, and that we cannot tell from them whether the real shape of the coin changes or not. They agree, that is, in accepting the Humean premise. Neither, therefore, can refute the other. Hence, Ayer believes that the dispute concerns a choice between two different languages or two ways of talking. It is the common premise which I dispute, and which I believe I have refuted in Chapters 5 and 6. If the appearance of the coin did not change as we moved, it would not be seen as a round coin retaining its shape and staying where it is – it is seen as one thing through the changing appearances. Far from there being any contradiction to resolve in this, to see anything is to see it as we see it, as it looks to us; we could not see things staying in place if they did not look different when seen from different places, and empirical knowledge, including the physics of rigid bodies, starts from this. Ayer's " sensible appearances " are simply the classic hypostatised looks, and about this there is indeed no dispute between Ayer and his interlocutor.

But at a later stage it is not the look which is taken to be the sense-datum. In his elaborate characterisation of sense-data – the point of which is to distinguish them as sharply as possible from things and eliminate the appearance and reality problem – Ayer discusses at some length various problems of perception, but only to insist that " in saying that there are sense-data I am not either assuming or rejecting any special empirical theory about the nature of what we observe ". They are not a species of material things – like Hume's perceptions they cannot have properties that they do not appear to have, or appear to have properties that they do not have. He then goes on to discuss the constancies of size, shape and colour.

We find that a man looks very much the same size at a distance of ten yards as at a distance of five. . . . We find that a white paper that is seen in the shadow of a screen does not appear the same colour as a black paper that is seen in a full light, even though the amount of light that the two papers reflect is the same. . . . And this constancy of appearances extends also to the shapes. Though philosophers seem inclined to assume that a round object, when it is seen obliquely, always looks elliptical, the empirical fact is that it usually does not. If I look sideways at a coin, the image that it projects upon my retina is indeed elliptical, but in spite of that, the coin still seems to me to be round. And by this I do not mean that, in spite of seeing it as elliptical, I judge the coin to be really round, but that it is a round and not an elliptical shape that I seem actually to see.

(*Foundations*, pp. 118–19)

Hence the sense-datum in question is not elliptical but *round*.

It is in cases where the fundamental problems are not merely verbal that the verbal problems tend to be intractable: the principal reason cited for using a sense-datum language is that it lays down " an unambiguous convention for the use of words that stands for modes of perception, freeing us from the verbal problems that develop, as we have seen, out of the ambiguous use of such words in ordinary speech" (*Foundations*, p. 26). But to talk of sense-data could at best only free us from the problems illustrated above by hiding them from us or preventing discussion of them. To say that a man looks very much the same size at a distance of ten yards as at a distance of five means this: we see him as being the same size at either distance, and indeed at fifty or one hundred yards, neither growing as he advances nor shrinking as he recedes. But if he did not *look* smaller as he got further away he would be seen as growing bigger the further away he got; and if he did not look bigger as he got nearer, he would be seen to shrink. Now what is constant is the size we see the man as being, not the way he looks or the way we see him at different distances. But the size of – so to speak – two man-like sense-data, Ayer decides in this case, is the size which in ordinary language we see the man as being, not the way he looks to us. Now in one sense of " looks ", to say a man looks smaller is to say he looks as if he were smaller or had shrunk: life-size waxworks are said to look smaller than life, that is, they seem to be smaller than life-size, or are seen as being smaller than life. But in the other sense of " looks ", to say a man looks smaller as he gets further away is not only compatible with, but inseparable from, his being seen as the same size; he does not visibly shrink, but he does get further away. Similarly in the case of the penny on the table at an oblique angle, Ayer's sense-datum is round, not elliptical. But a penny at an angle looks elliptical; if it did not look elliptical we should not see its roundness – a round penny lying flat on the table. If it looked round in the same sense, we would see it as an elliptical object. This is inseparable from seeing things in depth.

The problem for a sense-datum doctrine is to decide in any case what the datum is. But there is no answer to this question. There is no datum. If one were to ask Ayer whether his round sense-datum were not really elliptical, he would, without altering his position or moving the penny, have to admit that of course the penny looked elliptical, and that his sense-datum was now elliptical, and hence that it was a different sense-datum. But his object of perception would not have changed at all – it would still be there before him, and his actual experience, seeing as he would be in depth, would be of one thing, a round thing at an angle and therefore looking elliptical.

The proposal to adopt a sense-datum language and the belief that we can invent and use one if we please is inseparable from the Humean premise; to refute the premise is to destroy the proposal for a sense-datum language. Now Ayer agrees in a way that we do not actually have a sense-datum language, and that if we did we could not very well use it; but it would follow from his premise that there was nothing to prevent us from inventing one. What prevents us from doing so is that we wouldn't know what to refer to. So-called sense-datum statements have to be made, as Ayer notes, by reference to " material things ". This, however, is not due just to an accident of our upbringing whereby we happen already to have a " thing " language. Sense-datum statements have to be made by reference to things, because what they describe or express (badly) is the way these things look. We must refer to the things, simply because we see them. Such statements are not, in fact, in an alleged sense-datum language, but in ordinary language with the word sense-datum jammed in.

There is not one being who experiences and another who describes or expresses, but one who expresses his experience and what he experiences, who says with his tongue, teeth and lips, what he sees with his eyes, touches or grasps with his hands, and how he sees or feels it – how it looks or feels to him. The language fits our experience because it is our language. To invent another language for sense-experience would be to invent a language in which one could say only, if anything, what one can already say. Ayer admits and indeed emphasises this, but the proposal for a sense-datum language is founded on a mistake about the nature of sensible appearances, which is no less revealed in Ayer's ordinary language discussion. So far as sense-datum statements can be understood, they are ordinary language statements constructed in bizarre fashion about an otiose neologism. The view that our sense-experience may be spoken of and described in a way which is not one of the obvious, natural ways in our own language, nor yet a translation into another living language of one of these, nor yet an original expression such as a novelist or poet might invent, is founded on the classic premise that what is actually given to us in perception is " perceptions ", or sense-experiences, that is, that our sense-experience is not really as it is.

The issue concerns what Ayer might call a matter of fact. The issue is certainly whether his premise is true, and his argument for a sense-datum language depends upon this. But there is perhaps some reason to say that what is in dispute is not a matter of fact. Neither the reflexive analysis of experience nor the analysis of the language in which it is expressed is concerned with what are ordinarily called matters of fact. What we ordinarily call a matter of fact is what we, being as we are, can discover or infer to be the case in the world. We do this by observation, by looking and seeing and inferring from what we see, as embodied subjects. To discover what is the case, what the empirical facts are, is already to be an embodied subject in the world of things, events, and processes to be investigated. We know how our experience is, not by observing it – for it is not something in the world to be observed – but by having it; and we know what it is to be an embodied, seeing, hearing, talking subject, not by observing one, but by being one – we must be this to observe anything or say anything true or false about it. Now just as conceptual or linguistic analysis is the analysis of expressions which we already use meaningfully in actual situations and know what we mean by, so reflexive or phenomenological analysis is the analysis of experience which we already have – and not least, as we shall see, our having a language, for what an expression means in any context is what one of us, being as we are, with the experience we have, means by it.

What is at issue is not what is the case in the world but the nature of the experience whereby we can and do discover what is the case in the world. To hypostatise the looks of things and make the looks our objects is to make nonsense of our actual experience and wilfully to adopt a language in which no matter of empirical fact can ever be stated. We cannot find out or discover anything about a sense-datum or about a hundred sense-data, for there are no such objects. We cannot for instance measure a sense-datum, or the space between two sense-data. The sense-datum language if there were one, would not " enable us to refer to familiar facts in a clearer and more convenient way ". The " experience " it would refer to would be that of a disembodied awareness of free-floating looks.

Since in Ayer's view it is misleading to regard the question whether we see things or sense-data as a question of fact, one might suppose it was also misleading to regard the question whether sense-data exist or whether things exist as a question of fact. But the effect of adopting the sense-datum language is the adoption of the view that sense-data indubitably exist, but things do not indubitably exist: the Humean view. We are aware of sense-data and sense-data exist because this is how " sense-datum " is defined. " It is inconceivable ", says Ayer, " that any sense-datum should not be sensed veridically, since it has been made self-contradictory to say of an experienced sense-datum that it does not exist or that it does not really have the properties it appears to have." " As I use the word ' sense-datum ', to deny that there were sense-data would be to deny that anything ever was observed." (*Foundations*, p. 16.) Ayer might seem to be defining his object of direct awareness into existence, ensuring, as it were by fiat, that there is something for the term " sense-datum " to refer to. What he is doing, however, is not so fantastic as that; all that he has done is to define more carefully what he has all along taken for granted in the Humean way – the hypostatised " perception " which is indubitably given to consciousness and which is as it appears. Without this there would be no question at all of a sense-datum language.

It is by reason of the Humean dogma, likewise, that statements about material things " are never conclusively verifiable " (*Foundations*, p. 239). If one rejects the dogma, such statements are often of course quite conclusively verifiable in the only sense which in ordinary language this expression has. To verify the statement that the cat is in the kitchen, for example, I go to the kitchen and see it there on the mat playing with a ball of wool, lift it up, feel its soft furry warmth and hear it purring. The statement is thus conclusively verified. One might take it as a paradigm case. What else could " conclusively verifiable " mean? But if one adopts the Humean dogma and the sense-datum language which Ayer founds upon it, the verification of a statement about a " material thing " – such as a cat – would be its entailment by a set of statements about sense-data. Since no finite set of statements about sense-data can ever formally entail a statement about a material thing, such a statement can never be conclusively verified.

Now if the whole issue were simply which language to adopt, the ordinary language or the sense-datum language, it would be astonishing that our adopting the sense-datum language led us to deny what we are bound to assert, if we are sane, in the ordinary language, viz., that we can conclusively verify that the cat is in the kitchen. It is because the issue is not simply which language to use, but because it is assumed throughout that what is immediately given is " perceptions " and that of these alone can we be certain, that we are led to this astonishing consequence.

Apart from our embodied being in the midst of things, our seeing things over there from here, there is no sense in talking of looks or appearances, or indeed of talking about how to talk of them. It seems to make sense if they are called sense-data. For if we simply talk about looks or appearances we are at once committed to talk of seeing and what we see, as and how we see it, and we cannot do that without taking account of what seeing is actually like. But if we talk about sense-data, we can say that we sense them or are aware of them without saying how – without saying we see or hear or touch or handle or scrutinise and without thereby committing ourselves to recognise the existence of one " material thing " – our own embodied self. We can talk about sense-data in general, as Hume talks about perceptions in general. But in general only.

One of the reasons cited for using a sense-datum language is to free us " from the verbal problems that develop, as we have seen, out of the ambiguous use " of words that stand for modes of perception (*Foundations*, p. 26). That such problems do crop up we have seen in the case of the verb " to look ". They can be cleared up by considering carefully the contexts in which the allegedly ambiguous statements are made, as J. L. Austin has neatly and elegantly shown in *Sense and Sensibilia* (London: O.U.P., 1962). If words were not thus polyvalent we should need a much greater vocabulary. Misunderstandings arise more often in philosophical discussion than in practice. This results from thinking of words and sentences rather than what we mean when we say such-and-such in an actual situation; and this latter of course lands us in reflexive analysis of our actual experience, from which our actual language is inseparable. What the words mean is what we mean – we can explain ourselves.

Let me mention a few of the commonest distinctions relevant to the present topic. There is first the distinction between the way a house looks from here – the way I see it from here – and what I see it as, namely, an oblong house. What I see it as may not be what it is: I may see as the front of a house what is only a façade of boards, or I may see as a door in the wall what is only a *trompe-l'œil* painting of a door. And in these cases the things look *like* what I see them as. But I may see a thing as what in fact it is, but looking *like* something else: I may see a bare tree as such, but looking like a bunch of snakes writhing in the air, or I may see a man looking like an old woman. But all such expressions have to be understood in the situation in which they are used, for often one can be substituted for another.

For example, I might say I see the tree as a bunch of snakes when I mean, as above, " looking like a bunch of snakes ". If I said of some bovine character that I saw him as a great ox, this would not mean that I did not see him as a man – that I failed to recognise him as a man. Again, there are situations where to say something looks like a man and to say you see it as a man would amount to the same. The situation is essential to understanding what is meant. When we talk about the shape that something appears to have, we generally imply that we cannot make out what the shape is, that we can't see it properly. When we can see it properly, if we talk about the way it looks from here we are not then talking about the shape it has or appears to have.

The ambiguity of words and sentences out of context results from their flexibility – one of the fundamental characteristics of a living language – which is not only compatible with but essential to contextual precision. If a problem is purely verbal it is not much of a problem. Ayer claims for example, that there are two senses of " perceive " – by which he seems to mean " see " – and in one of these senses it can be used in such a way " that to say of an object that it is perceived does not entail saying that it exists in any sense at all ". The context in which he asserts this (*Foundations*, p. 21) is a discussion of seeing something double or, as people say, seeing two things when there is only one.

This problem is not a verbal one. The problem is to analyse the difference between seeing one man double and seeing twins, a difference of which we are all aware. The analysis of this difference is of some importance for realising how in ordinary seeing we fixate and order things in their spatial relations. Merleau-Ponty has done this very well.[1] In double vision, the two " images " do not have a place in the world but float as it were in front of things. When we fixate or look at the object they withdraw into it. This fixation is not automatic but intentional, that is to say, we look at the object. The two " images " are not objects and we cannot look at them. To look and see is to see the object, one thing.

I have not dealt with Ayer's introductory discussion of the " argument from illusion ", since Ayer's Humean dogma is in my view the

[1] ' Le Sentir ', *La Phénoménologie de la perception*, pp. 267–9.

real premise of his argument for the sense-datum language. But I must say the alleged illusions are an odd lot. I cite only one example: there are, we are told, " complete hallucinations, such as the mirage " (*Foundations*, p. 3). Now in fact anyone with normal vision can *see* a mirage. To take it for an oasis or a ship at sea is a mistake, but it is no more a hallucination than to take a bush by the roadside on a dark night for a crouching figure. The point about hallucinations is that there is nothing to see. J. L. Austin has already dealt with other " illusions " in this section in his *Sense and Sensibilia*.

CHAPTER SIXTEEN

LANGUAGE AND EXPERIENCE

THE empiricist concept of sense-experience has often been defended by saying that it is useful theoretically to isolate or abstract what we get by the senses from what we make of it, to abstract what is given from our " interpretation " of it. And this sort of talk is very common in psychology text-books. But this defence simply assumes the point at issue. For if we are talking about actual experience, we get whatever we get as we get it. Interpretation and inference start from what we actually see and hear. If what we saw and heard already incorporated our interpretation and inference, the concepts of evidence and of observational data would be vacuous and all witnesses would be unreliable. As we all know, however, reliable witnesses are those who say what they saw and heard and do not impose their own interpretations and inferences upon it.

What underlies the interpretation story is simply the fact that whatever we see or hear, we see or hear as such-and-such, or as is sometimes said, under a certain description. And different people see or hear the same thing under different descriptions. Whereas I see merely some curious marks, a hunter sees the tracks of a rabbit, or what look like the tracks of a rabbit. Whereas I hear a joke (in English), a Spanish peasant hears a strange-sounding utterance in a foreign tongue. But the hunter and I see the same thing (I see him looking at it), and the peasant and I hear the same thing; what I see as marks on the ground, the hunter sees as rabbit tracks, and what I hear as a joke, the peasant hears as strange words. There is no difficulty for us in telling each other what we see the marks as, or what we hear the sounds as, or in understanding each other. What we can never do is to say what it is we see as marks or tracks or hear as sounds or as a joke. " This ", as Aristotle said, is always " such " – the universal *in re*. The matter is the matter of the form, and the form is the form of the matter. The matter *as such* would be the form of itself.

There is no conflict between what the hunter says he sees and what I see – I understand him perfectly and may take his word for it that these *are* rabbit tracks – nor is there any conflict between what the peasant says he hears and what I hear: we should all be perfectly reliable witnesses and, indeed, mutually confirming witnesses. For we have not imposed any interpretation on what we saw or heard and all our descriptions are true.

There is no need to insist that with increasing experience and familiarity we see things " with different eyes ", or hear sounds, one might say, " with different ears ". To hear a tune a second time is to hear it differently. There is, however, the utmost need to insist that we never see or hear anything except as such-and-such, under a certain description.

Empiricists have discussed at length how sense-experience should be spoken of and described, and have distinguished the meanings of terms in which we do so, but remarkably few have discussed our sense-experience of language, and this is intimately connected with the fact that from Hume to Ayer the sense-experience they discuss is overwhelmingly visual. Sense-experience, it is understood, is of colours and shapes – perhaps solid objects, if you insist. Of course, they say, there are sounds and smells and tastes and textures, but we need not bother with these. Nor with pushes and pulls and bumps.

Our sense-experience, on this view, does not include our hearing funny stories, threats, songs, voices like saws, loving murmurs, or witty remarks. The convention is that though sense-experience enters into all that, there is much more to it than sense-experience. This may seem reasonable. But it is precisely the same argument as before: the loving murmur or the witty remark is not what we get by the senses, but what we make of what we get. And as before we must reply: very well, we know what we make of it, what we hear it as; what then is it that we hear *as* a loving murmur or a witty remark? Sounds? But we do not hear sounds just as sounds of no description; that is not what we experience. Of course witty remarks *are* sounds – if they were not, we would not hear them. But we hear them as witty remarks, not bells tolling, or dogs barking: that is the sort of sounds they are. And that is why in the common language witty remarks and loving murmurs are among the innumerable things we are said to hear. The sounds of our own language are only heard as sounds (though of a certain description, for example, the sound of voices talking) when we cannot hear what the speakers are saying. And this is closely analogous to the case where we see a dark shape in the twilight but cannot make out what it is.

The only use I can see for the term "sense-experience" is simply to refer compendiously to seeing, hearing, touching, etc. For the empiricist concepts of the senses and of sense-experience, I see no use at all. These concepts are governed by the sensationalist heritage: it is clear that the objection to regarding witty remarks as matters of sense-experience – as what we actually hear – is similar to the objection to regarding the wicked twinkle in someone's eye as a matter of sense-experience – as what we actually see. It is based on the view that what we really, "strictly" speaking, see or hear, or are aware of, is some sort of data, and not what we suppose we see or hear. And this view amounts to saying that experience is not really as it is.

To understand this, we must return to the origins of the doctrine. Sounds are events which occur when a pressure wave within a certain range of frequencies impinges on the tympanum, etc. Since that is all we get, what we think we hear (a witty remark) is not what we really hear. To explain what we think we hear and *say* we hear, there are the unconscious interpretation story and other philosophical fictions. But these constitute an admission that we do not actually experience what we are alleged to experience.

The emphasis with which generations of empiricists and others have asserted that sight is by far the most important sense for those who have it is due, I think, not simply to the fact that people have a greater horror of being blind than of being deaf. It is due also to the fact that when language is functioning effectively it passes unnoticed and is forgotten. What we hear the sounds *as*, is the meaning. It is on our lips and all about us from morning to night, but we do not hear it as sounds or even as words, but as meanings – information, funny stories, sentiments, compliments, insults, appeals, demands, etc. The meaning, as Merleau-Ponty says, devours the sign.

It is not surprising that reading does not count as sense-experience either, according to the traditional concept. Seeing the marks on the page would count, but not reading – reading is an interpretation of the marks. But this is not the experience of one who can read. We do not see the marks and interpret them. We do not see the marks as such at all. To read is to see the meaning on the page. It is not in the margin or somewhere off the page, but there, accumulating from line to line and page to page. We look at the *Treatise* not to see the print, but to see what Hume says. Reading, in the intellectualist view which is happily at ease with the sensationalist account of perception, is an operation of the intellect translating symbols into concepts. After all, there are only black marks on the white page; that is all there is to see; what the illiterate sees is what we all see. To this the answer is as before: yes, but he does not see them *as* what we see them *as* when we are actually reading. We have difficulty in seeing the marks *as* marks or the letters as letters, in *not* seeing them as words and meanings and in *not* reading them. We notice print of a particular fount mainly when we've never seen it before.

Language is taken for granted as one's own body is taken for granted. We rarely attend to it and notice it. And as philosophers have so often forgotten or actually denied in their discussions of " physical objects " and bodies, that of one body they have uniquely the experience not merely of perceiving it but of being it, so they have also forgotten that they have the experience of speaking and of being articulate. If they were less articulate, they might not have forgotten it so readily. To be articulate is part of being embodied. One must already be articulate to say anything about language or anything else. The embodied subject is *a priori* in this as in other respects.

The language which we learn is, like every other aspect of the world in which we find ourselves, already there before us, with all its categories and meanings: in learning these we learn to distinguish, sort out, and relate things. To learn a language is to learn to make sense of the world. We incorporate our native language by spontaneous mimicry, like other bodily skills. In hearing and saying in a lived situation, the child is making sense, not only of what he hears and says, but of the situation. In a similar way we learn a foreign language well by making it ours; we take possession of it or are possessed by it, like the actor by his spoken rôle. We must do without explanation or interpretation, suspend our own language, so that this other language can make its own sense in its own terms for us. We install ourselves in it as a new way of " living the world ".

The world as we express or describe it is inseparable from the world itself. Thus the distinction between the fact and the statement, the real and the true, the state of affairs and the description of it, always tends to disappear. Our experience is not separable from our power to say, to express and to describe. Everything can be said, and what is difficult to say is difficult to understand. To be at a loss for words is to be at a loss *tout court*, to be unable to make sense of the situation. To find the words is to begin to make sense of it and cope with it, whether we do this by exclamation, ritual or incantation, or by objective description.

This skill is unique, but like all other skills it cannot be understood in isolation from our being in the world as embodied subjects. What we mean or think has no existence apart from its being said. Without saying, we do not know what we think or mean, or, what is the same thing, we have not effectively thought or meant it. Talking is thinking aloud; silent thinking is unvoiced talking.

Even in thinking aloud or in hearing what others say we do not have the experience of producing or hearing these curious sounds we make. For the sounds are uttered or heard as meanings. In listening to someone we hear his meaning, make it ours or reject it, and in talking we simply think or mean aloud.

Not only do we not notice the movements of our tongue, teeth and lips – the point of any bodily skill once acquired is that we can count on it and use it, but do not think of it – we do not ordinarily notice our own words or turns of expression. It is when we fail to follow someone or he fails to follow us, that we attend to the words and try, as it were, to spell out the meaning. We also attend to the words when we are putting on some sort of performance, and we frequently do so in writing. When we cannot find the words, however, it is a mistake to suppose that the thought or meaning is, as it were, ready and waiting for the right vehicle: finding the words *is* thinking.

In ordinary talk, unstudied utterance, as Ryle happily calls it, the words are self-effacing. And they are so *a fortiori* in silent thinking, the least " studied " of all, since we are not communicating it to anyone and have no need to make our meaning understood. It is thus easy to believe that our thinking can be wordless. Hence no doubt the classic view that our thinking has a purely external and contingent relation to words, to our being articulate, and to our being bodies. The illusion of wordless thought is central to the classic mind–body dualism.

In the rationalist tradition, meanings are abstracted from words, and as concepts or universals or essences are regarded as existing or sub-sisting independently of anyone's thinking them or having them. When anyone does think them or have them, it is his mind that has them or his intellect that apprehends them, and only *per accidens* are they symbolised and conveyed in sensible sounds or marks. The bodily skill or articulation, the fruit of incessant early practice, which constitutes the possession of a language and is inseparable from the ability to think, has no place in this account of the mind and its con-cepts.

Nor does it have any place in the classic empiricist-nominalist account. In the Humean doctrine, ideas – copies of impressions – are required to do service as concepts or meanings. But they cannot. Words are themselves impressions and ideas, occurring and becoming associated with other sorts of impressions and ideas. They refer but they have no sense or meaning. And the effect of dualism in Hume, as I have earlier noted, is to reduce all doing to perceiving, and this must apply also to talking and saying, of which no account is to be found in his work. Words, it would seem, are heard but not uttered.

The dualist account of thinking is no different from the dualist account of volition, which is indeed a kind of thinking, an act of mind. Just as the volition is an occurrence prior to the overt happenings – movements of a body – with which it has a purely external and con-tingent relation, so thinking is a mental act which has a purely external relation with formulation or symbolisation in sounds or marks, and it might seem, none at all with being a body and articulating with tongue, teeth and lips. The *Cogito* hence must be silent.

But to say " cogito " is not to have perceptions or ideas (of saying with tongue, teeth and lips) but to be a body articulating one's meaning. To do anything, and not least to talk, is not to be passively conscious of events or happenings or aware of one's body or vocal organs as objects of contemplation. Unless one is a body, one cannot do anything: " doing " means " doing bodily ", and the experience of talking no less than any other is a bodily experience. We do not put what we think or mean into words; our meaning is only realised in the words. To think what one is going to say is to say it to oneself.

The language is the common inheritance. But to enter upon it and possess it is to incarnate it as one's power of meaning, thinking and saying. It is easy to regard it as a thing with a life and development of its own, like the body politic or the nation, something as it were apart from those who speak it. This is the way some conceptual analysts treat it. And likewise any word or expression can be regarded as independent of what anyone means or hears. But a language is only the deposit of acts of meaning: it exists only in being uttered, heard, and repeated, created and re-created.

In the objective study of language, as it is conducted by some semanticists, a curious problem arises: what to make of meaning. W. V. O. Quine, who has himself been much concerned with this problem and inclines to a behaviourist view, has put the matter thus:

> Pending a satisfactory explanation of the notion of meaning, linguistics in semantic fields are in the situation of not knowing what they are talking about. This is not an untenable situation. Ancient astronomers knew the movements of the planets remarkably well without knowing what sort of things the planets were. But it is a theoretically unsatisfactory situation. . . .[1]

The analogy drawn by Quine between the problem of what a planet is and the problem of what a meaning is, is bizarre, to say the least. But the difficulty concerning the nature of meaning is a familiar

[1] *From a Logical Point of View*, p. 47.

155

one for behaviourism and indeed for any study which attempts to reduce the embodied subject to some sort of object. Meaning is no mystery for anyone who is articulate and effectively says what he means. The problem arises when the embodied subject is objectivised.

Linguistic analysis, as practised by J. L. Austin, takes our possession of a language for granted. It consists of reflexive analysis of what one means. The *O.E.D.* was not Austin's Bible, as is sometimes said. It was an *aide-mémoire*. The question is always: " What do I mean when I say . . .? ", " What do I mean by . . .? " Only someone who is in possession of the language can answer that or know whether an analysis is correct or incorrect. To analyse the meaning is to analyse one's own meaning.

CHAPTER SEVENTEEN

PHYSICALISM AND PHENOMENALISM

IF one may generalise about the Vienna circle, their common standpoint was essentially that of a neutral monism similar to Russell's, founded upon the doctrine of sensations which they inherited from Ernst Mach. The idea of a logical construction was intimately related to that of a unified science. In the logical language, physical statements would be translatable or transformable into psychological statements or, as Schlick put it, " propositions concerning bodies are transformable into equivalent propositions concerning the occurrence of sensations in accordance with laws " (*Logical Positivism*, ed. A. J. Ayer, p. 107). The unification of science in this way was philosophy.

In *The Logical Construction of the World*, Carnap's first problem is that of the data or ground elements which are to be values of the variables, whereby alone his construction is not merely logical but a logical construction of the world. Acceptance of his system depends upon acceptance of his argument for the subjectless *Erlebnis* which he takes for " quasi-analysis ". Carnap seems to insist that this is some sort of raw reality – a transverse slice of the stream of experience.

This question is discussed lucidly by Nelson Goodman in his book *The Structure of Appearance*. Goodman argues, to my mind conclusively, that for the purpose of a logical construction what is given, in the sense of being a " raw datum ", is irrelevant. But while Goodman is right as opposed to Carnap, he seems to me to be wrong in a more fundamental way owing to a preconception about sense-experience which he shares with many other empiricists. His own suggested system takes " qualia " as its atoms, and includes places and times among the qualia. In no sense are these supposed to be the units

" in which experience is originally given ". Other systems with other units are entirely admissible, and one system could be preferred to another only on grounds of utility.[1] There is no question of the qualia " floating free " of concreta; all concreta contain qualia and all erlebs contain concreta. It is pointless to ask which sort of unit comes first or which is *really* fundamental. If the question is " which way experience is packaged on original delivery ", says Goodman, " I have no idea what criteria would be applied in seeking an answer." A constructional system is not necessarily intended as " an epistemological history " (*The Structure of Appearance*, pp. 150–1).

Now Goodman is certainly right to reject any notion of " raw " or " original " experience, but the worst difficulty is one which is raised no less by his system than by Carnap's. It is the difficulty of knowing what is meant by quale or a concretum or an erleb, a difficulty akin to that of knowing what Ayer means by a sense-datum. It should be specified in the ordinary language so that there is no doubt what is referred to. But this is not done, and the reason again lies in the nature of language and experience. One can talk about the world and any-thing whatever in the world, or one can talk of one's experience of this and that, but one cannot talk as if there were no distinction between experience and what is experienced, or between what is experienced as it is experienced and what is experienced as it actually is. Now this is not a matter of epistemological history or of " which way experience is packaged on original delivery " – what that would mean is as obscure to me as it is to Goodman. It is a matter of the way we have it now.

If anything could be said to be packaged it would be what was experienced, not the experience of it, and this is precisely the distinction which Goodman does not make. As in all such systems, experience is identified with what is experienced. The qualia, concreta and erlebs are not what we see or hear, nor yet our hearing and seeing, but both or neither. It is another " subjectless " system. But Goodman almost certainly would want to deny his commitment to any view about the nature of experience. It is necessary therefore to show that he has such a view and what this view is. For this purpose I take his discussion of the question of " epistemological priority " in connection with the

[1] I do not know what utility such systems have.

respective claims of physicalism and phenomenalism, which, as he remarks, is badly confused.

The claim is that one basis corresponds more closely than another to what is directly apprehended or immediately given, that one more nearly than the other represents naked experience as it comes to us – prior to analysis, inference, interpretation, conceptualisation. Now one may certainly ask whether a given description is *true* of what is experienced; but here the further question is whether one or the other of two *true* descriptions more faithfully describes what is experienced *as it is experienced* – and this I have some difficulty in understanding. What I saw a moment ago might be described as a moving patch of red, as a cardinal bird, or as the thirty-seventh bird in the tree this morning; and all these descriptions may be true. But the phenomenalist seems to hold that what I saw I saw *as* a moving patch of red, which I then interpreted as a glimpse of a cardinal bird. The physicalist seems to hold that I saw it *as* a cardinal bird, and only by analysis reached the description of it as a moving patch of red. Both apparently agree (since I made no count) that what I saw I did not see *as* the thirty-seventh bird in the tree this morning. Now just what is in question here? Let me try to formulate it. . . .

. . . The criterion suggested here is apparently that what I see, I see as what I know it to be at the moment I see it. Did I then see [it] . . . as more than 5000 miles from China, as weighing less than Aristotle, etc. . . . surely this formulation will not do.

Perhaps, then . . . to say I saw a red thing is nearer to my raw experience than to say I saw a red bird, and this in turn is nearer than to say I saw the eighth red bird on the tree this morning. In that case I am more faithful to my experience if I describe what I saw as a vertebrate than as a bird, and faithful to the ultimate degree if I describe it as a cow-or-non-cow.

(Appearance, pp. 103 ff.)

Goodman's purpose is to show the difficulty of " rating perceptible individuals on a scale of immediacy ", and to show that the claim of greater immediacy for either a physicalistic or a phenomenalistic basis is not easily sustained. He is entirely successful in this. But he goes on to say that " an economic and well-constructed system of either sort " will do and that it need not be further justified in terms of " some subtle epistemological or metaphysical hierarchy ". In applying the terms " phenomenal " and " physical ", he says, he is not attempting to distinguish the immediate and the non-immediate: " For example, the two-dimensional field of vision is clearly different from three-dimensional physical space; a change of position in either may or may not be accompanied by a change of position in the other." The belief of empiricists that they do not " immediately " see in depth seems irremediable.

Goodman confuses the meaningless question about " naked experience " with an entirely different question: " Whether one or the other of two *true* descriptions more faithfully describes what is experienced as it is experienced "; and this he says he has some difficulty in understanding. This difficulty stems from the failure to make the ordinary distinction between what there is, or what is the case, and our experience of it at any particular time. What is the case can only be known by experience, but a true statement of someone's experience need not be a true statement of what is the case. If I see an attendant in Madame Tussaud's as one of the exhibits, this is a true description of what I see as I see it, but not of what I see as it really is – not a waxwork but a man. I see something, but I see it as a waxwork when it is actually a man. There is no difficulty in understanding this.

Now Goodman holds that a true description is a description of what objectively, empirically, is the case, and holds further that such a description can be given either in physicalist or in phenomenalist terms as he describes these. But this is not so, for different sorts of descriptions are in question – though none of them is a description of occurrences in a two-dimensional " field of vision ". One might say the phenomenalist prefers the looks of things, while the physicalist prefers the things. Ordinary language, since experience is as it is, has to have both; a thing seen in depth is seen from an angle, looking as it looks, and if it looks very odd then it looks very odd, whether or not it *is* in any sense odd or unusual. The question is what one means, what one is describing.

Now Goodman's assumption is that all true descriptions are descriptions of what is the case objectively; they are all empirical descriptions, descriptions of what is observed. But this is not so. Descriptions of a thing are objective; descriptions of seeing it or of how one sees it are not. One does not see or observe one's seeing, what one sees is the thing. One knows that there is a cat on the mat by seeing the cat on the mat. One does not know one sees it by seeing or observing one's seeing it. Observing is the condition of making an empirical, objective statement. Such statements are made about what is observed or observable. One does not observe one's observing, one's hearing or feeling or thinking, in a word, one's experience. It is by experience that one determines what is the case, objectively. But objective statements are not statements about one's experience, but statements of what is the case in the world.

To misunderstand this is to misunderstand the nature of scientific experiment and discovery. It proceeds on the *a priori* assumption that there is a world which is as it is independently of anyone's knowing it as it is, but which can be known by observation and experiment. That is the very meaning of discovery. The looks of things or the way you see things or I see things are not objects of scientific determination and discovery. They look the way they look, but the way they look to me may be very different from the way they look to you. Looks are not objective. They may be described and they may be depicted but they cannot be objectively determined by measurement. Nor can a collection of looks constitute a thing.

Underlying Goodman's difficulty is the sensationalist heritage. He rightly realises that nothing can intelligibly be said about raw data of perception. But he assumes that there are, or were, such data. Since we cannot describe the data, all we can describe is what is the case in the world, which we may do in many different ways; all such statements will be empirical and will be true or false by exactly the same criteria. If he is not saying that what we describe truly is what is the case in the world, the answer is: then it can only be our subjective experience. Goodman does not make the distinction. It is all one to him. Yet it is evident that " A cardinal bird flew in a south-westerly direction across the garden at 11.36 a.m. " would *not* be a true description of my experience as I sat reading and something red caught my eye. It might be a true statement, but not of my experience. There is no great difficulty in describing present experience as we have it. Such descriptions are among the most frequent and commonplace in the language. It is impossible to believe that Goodman does not use them with perfect ease when he is not writing books, or that his descriptions are not effortlessly true descriptions.

A birdwatcher looking for cardinal birds and knowing what they look like, might say as he sees the red flash across the garden, " There's one! ", if that is the way such a bird looks in flight. He may, of course, be wrong. He would follow it up and try to get a clear sight of it with his binoculars. I, who don't know what a cardinal bird looks like in flight or otherwise, might say: " What was that red thing flashing across? " And this, in the form of a question, would express my experience better than the statement that I saw something red flashing across, for it says not only that, but that I wonder what it was. "What's that?" is what we say when, for example, some sudden movement arrests our attention, but we couldn't get a proper look at it. A perfectly familiar experience. If the bird landed on a tree in view we should scrutinise it, try to see as much as possible. But if it flashed across and disappeared, we should be " left hanging ", unsatisfied, and " What was that? " would simply express this. If one were feeling drowsy, one might not be very curious, unless some- one else roused one's attention. A true description of one's experience then would be something like; " Yes, I did see something red there, but I was just dropping off." What this describes is not a cardinal bird in flight, as it might be described by an ornithologist. There is simply no question of that; it is not that sort of description, for one does not know what it was one saw – and one knows very well one doesn't know – one didn't have a chance to get a look at it. But there is no question either of naked or raw experience, whatever that would be, nor of epistemological history, whatever that would be. Simply a question of our actual experience, easily and truly expressible in un- studied utterance.

Goodman's problem arises because he does not distinguish between what objectively happens in the world and how we experience what is within our purview at any particular time and place, in our situation, our mood, with our preoccupations and interests. He is committed philosophically to the same preconceptions about sense-experience as those whose views he is criticising; he realises, as some of them have failed to do, that there is no question of what is really or originally given, that this notion is vacuous; but he will admit only one sort of true description. But as everyone knows, there are innumerable cases where we don't know what " it " objectively is, and that is why we ask questions. If we glimpse something red, that is our experience, but we don't know what the something is. And that is the difference between a description of our perceptual experience and what is objectively the case.

There is one fundamental point about our perceptual experience on which I have touched several times, and which is worth making again in connection with Goodman's rejection of " naked " or " raw " experience. It is that when we catch a glimpse of anything, as for example the patch of red flashing across the garden, we look at it to make out what it is – to determine it as such-and-such in the world. Perception has its teleology, as Merleau-Ponty says, its end is the thing " in person " or " in the flesh ". It passes from the indeterminate to the determinate.

Now much that is described in the phenomenalist way – " a patch of red " or " a red patch moving across " – is a merely transitory stage in the progress of perception to its end, or, if you like, in the emergence of the determinate thing. It is not what we finally see, for seeing is the end of looking; it is what we look at, seek with the gaze, before we have seen it properly and got a good sight of it. It is nothing determinate, but indeterminate, and cannot therefore be described except as " moving red ", that is to say, not as anything in the world, for among the things in the world there are no mere " moving reds ", discarnate qualities whizzing about. A moving red what? The answer to that is what we look for.

Experience of the indeterminate is common, but the point is that it is entirely artificial to attempt to describe in detail the indeterminate, for to attempt to describe anything seriously is first to take a good look and determine it, see what we can of it. Things themselves, we assume, are in themselves determinate, but, as Merleau-Ponty argues very powerfully, they are first constituted as determinate by the teleology of perception passing by looking from the indeterminate to the determinate. What *is* determinate, he argues, is essentially what *has been* or could be determined. Though we see the green book at the edge of the desk vaguely, we assume that it is not in itself vague, for to look at it would be to see it properly, to see its hard, firm contours. When our eyes leave it, roving over and dominating the things in our purview, having been once determined, it remains determinate for us in itself, and even behind our back, or when we go out of the room.

CHAPTER EIGHTEEN

CAUSAL EXPLANATION AND THE MECHANIST BOGY

THE primordial thesis, unreasoned, unargued, on which all enquiry and investigation and discovery is founded, is that there is a world and that it is in itself, independent of our being in it, and of our seeing anything of it or knowing anything about it. To ask "What is the world?" is to ask "What is it that there is?" All we can say of the world is what we know about this or that aspect of it. But there is always more. It is thus perfectly true that when we speak of the world we do not know what we are talking about, as we do when we speak of the dining-room table or the United States or the House of Commons. The world is not an object and not determinable as an object; what is known or what is determined or determinable is in the world. It is by virtue of the primordial thesis of the world that we always believe there is more to know, that there are facts, not yet, but to be, known.

All our experience incorporates this thesis. We find what is there, already there, waiting as it were to be scrutinised, examined, discovered, or used and shaped for our ends. It is given in the sense that we do not invent it – that is the only sense in which there is a datum. What we make, we make of what we find. What we see is to be further explored and determined. To see anything is to begin, at least, to determine what it is. The thesis that knowledge is possible is no less primordial, unargued, and unreasoned, than the thesis of the world: it is in every look we cast on anything, every scrutiny, every question. The thesis of the world and the thesis that it is to be known are not matters of knowledge, but presupposed in all enquiry and all discovery of what is the case, the way things are.

Hume realised this and his doctrine of natural belief is an expression of it. But while recognising its non-rational character, he attempted to give an account of it in naturalistic terms, terms which presuppose it. Some of his successors have tried to treat the world as consisting of permanent possibilities of sensations. Gilbert Ryle is not the philosopher of whom one would most readily think in this connection, but the dispositional analysis of properties in the form in which he presents it leads, I think, straight into this position.

There are [says Ryle] at least two quite different senses in which an occurrence is said to be 'explained'; and there are correspondingly at least two quite different senses in which we ask 'why' it occurred and two quite different senses in which we say that it happened 'because' so and so was the case. The first sense is the causal sense. To ask why the glass broke is to ask what caused it to break, and we explain, in this sense, the fracture of the glass when we report that a stone hit it. The 'because' clause in the explanation reports an event, namely the event which stood to the fracture of the glass as cause to effect.

But very frequently we look for and get explanations of occurrences in another sense of 'explanation'. We ask why the glass shivered when struck by the stone and we get the answer that it was because the glass was brittle. Now 'brittle' is a dispositional adjective; that is to say, to describe the glass as brittle is to assert a general hypothetical proposition about the glass. So when we say that the glass broke when struck because it was brittle, the 'because' clause does not report a happening or a cause; it states a law-like proposition. People commonly say of explanations of this second kind that they give the 'reason' for the glass breaking when struck.

How does the law-like general hypothetical proposition work? It says, roughly, that the glass, *if* sharply struck or twisted, etc., *would* not dissolve or stretch or evaporate but fly into fragments. The matter of fact that the glass did at a particular moment fly into fragments, when struck by a particular stone, is explained, in this sense of 'explain', when the first happening, namely the impact of the stone, satisfies the protasis of the general hypothetical proposition, and when the second happening, namely the fragmentation of the glass, satisfies its apodosis.

(*Concept*, pp. 88–9)

There is [says Ryle] at our disposal an indefinitely wide range of dispositional terms for talking about things, living creatures and human beings. Some of these can be applied indifferently to all sorts of things; for example, some pieces of metal, some fishes, and some human beings weigh 140 lb., are elastic and combustible, and all of them, if left unsupported, fall at the same rate of acceleration. Other dispositional terms can be applied only to certain kinds of things: 'hibernates', for example, can be applied with truth or falsity only to living creatures, and 'Tory' can be applied with truth or falsity only to non-idiotic, non-infantile, non-barbarous human beings. . . .

(*Concept*, pp. 125–6)

According to Ryle's account, if we ask why the glass shattered when struck and receive the answer " because it was brittle ", this means " if it were struck it would shatter ". Since *ex hypothesi* we have just seen this happening, in what sense could this be said to be an explanation of any sort? (This would be like Molière's *vertu dormitive*.) It is true that if glass is brittle it will shatter when struck with a suitable thing, and this is the main way in which we discover that things are brittle. But to ascribe this property to it is not to say anything about how the property is discovered. To say it shattered because it was brittle is to say it shattered because it was a certain sort of thing: to say it was brittle is to give a causal explanation of its shattering no less than to say it shattered because it was struck, or because the stone was hard, heavy, and travelling fast, or because any other condition of its shattering was fulfilled. There are not two different senses of " because ", only one of which is causal, but several causes or causal conditions of the glass shattering. The " because " clause does report a cause in each case. People commonly use the word " reason " instead of " cause ", whether the cause in question is a property or an occurrence, but this is of no special importance or significance. This is very obvious in, for example, a causal account of the growth of plants: a whole complex of conditions must be specified.

The difference between tough glass and brittle glass lies in their molecular structure and the cause of this may be said to lie in the process of manufacture. This is no less a cause of glass breaking or not breaking when a stone hits it than is the throwing or impact of the stone. People who know nothing of molecular structure take brittleness to be a property of glass, and suppose that there is an inherent difference between tough and brittle materials which causes the one to shatter and the other not to shatter when struck. Similarly, it was assumed when the first Comet jet exploded in mid-air that there was some defect of the fuselage which caused it to disintegrate. This was found to be what is called metal fatigue, a condition which develops under prolonged stress in some alloys.

The point may be illustrated by another example. The cause of an explosion in a factory might be said to be a cigarette-end, or it might be said to be someone's putting the explosive material, months before the event, in the place where the cigarette-end lands. In an enquiry into the causes of an accidental explosion, they would equally be regarded as causes of the explosion. The dangerous condition of the factory, the disposition of the factory to explode, would be simply the explosive lying in that place. Its being there and the cigarette-end being thrown would be equally causes of the explosion. To say the glass broke because it was brittle is analogous to saying the factory exploded because it was in a dangerous condition: in the one case we may know what the condition was in some detail, and in the other not, but it is correctly assumed by people who know nothing of the nature of brittleness that there is something about the glass which makes it break easily. But for this, physical and chemical enquiry would have remained in their infancy. No one would have asked what the difference was between glass that broke easily and glass that didn't, for they would have thought that *was* the difference, and there was no more to be said.

Now if the enquiry into the causes of such commonplace events as the breaking of glass be carried further, there are of course many other causal conditions with which everyone is familiar. It depends for example upon thickness and weight in relation to the missile. What the law-like general proposition says " roughly " is too rough – it masks the fact that the weight of the glass, whereby it is where it is and not floating around, can with as much or as little reason be considered a dispositional property. And with as much or as little reason, it can be said that to say the glass is heavy is to state one or more general hypothetical propositions. And so for its mass, volume, thickness, roughness or smoothness, transparency and so on. To say the glass broke because it was brittle is a statement of exactly the same type as to say that it broke because it was thin or did not break because it was thick. Thickness happens to be a property which is visible to the naked eye. But no one supposes that all present properties whereby the present glass is glass are visible or evident at a glance.

Properties are causal conditions of happenings, events, processes and behaviour. To say they are dispositional is another way of saying this, and perfectly harmless if this is understood. Explanation in terms of properties is causal explanation. But if one says that " to describe glass as brittle is to assert a general hypothetical proposition about the glass " one has to say that to describe the glass as anything whatever is to assert a general hypothetical proposition. What, then, is the glass about which these general hypothetical propositions are asserted? The only way of saying what the glass is, is to say what properties it has. Its having these properties is its being glass; apart from them it is not glass, but, if anything, something else. To say it is glass is to say it has the properties of glass. If this is to assert general hypothetical propositions, to say it is glass is to do so, and to say that there is any glass in the world is to do so.

Ryle's view of dispositional properties as translatable into hypothetical propositions is inseparable from the view that any statement asserting what is not at present observable by the speaker is reducible to, and indeed identifiable with, one or more hypothetical propositions specifying the conditions or method of verification. It remains to show that this is not the meaning of such statements, but that such statements mean precisely what they appear to mean: that such-and-such is now actually the case, and that they are not really "if . . . then . . . " statements.

There is no dispute about how such statements are to be verified. The statement " There is a brown leather armchair in the next room " can be verified by going to the next room and seeing if there is such an armchair there. But " There is a brown leather armchair in the next room " does not mean " If I go to the next room, then I shall see, or be in a position to see, a brown leather armchair ", or any other statement saying in effect how the first statement is to be verified. For any such statement must specify the place where the observation could be made. Now to say *where* is to say there is such a place. But places are spatial determinations of what there is at them, or in them, or near them, or far from them, and no place can be mentioned or specified without a reference to something of which it is a spatial determination; all such determinations are relational – " here ", " there " and " elsewhere " are all correlative terms. For there to be places and times there has to be a world. When it is stated that there is a brown leather armchair in the next room, what is meant is that now at this moment there is a room next door and in it such a chair. To ascertain whether this is so, one must go thither from here. If there were not a world and things in the world, it could not be ascertained, for one would not, to put it crudely, know where to go to make the observation, for the place referred to in the hypothetical could not be said to exist. But the hypothetical proposition assumes the present existence of the next room and whatever is in it. It is because we take the independent existence of the world and everything in it for granted that we can formulate such hypotheticals. And it is because we take the existence of a piece of glass to be the existence of all the properties of the glass that we can formulate any hypothetical proposition about it. It is because it is what it is, or has the properties it has, that it behaves as it does in this or that circumstance. And this is part and parcel of causal explanation whether at the kitchen or at the laboratory level of sophistication.

This is very evident if one takes things which are actually named by their principal dispositional property, for example, high explosives. What constitutes the explosiveness of the explosive is its present chemical composition, and if it exploded it would be this no less than the dunt or the match which caused the explosion. It would explode, for example, because it was T.N.T. To say that it is T.N.T. and that T.N.T. is a high explosive is to describe a present existent. But to describe a present existent and ascribe properties to it is not, as Ryle suggests, to report any occult occurrences behind the scene; it is to say what sort of stuff it is, what, for example, its chemical composition is. There is nothing occult about this.

There is no harm, I repeat, in regarding properties as dispositional, if it is remembered that this is to regard them as causal conditions of various types of happenings or events. Now Ryle is concerned to show that " he boasted from vanity " is an explanation of the same type as " the glass broke because it was brittle ". If it is, it is a causal explanation as this is understood in the kitchen, the workshop and the laboratory.

> Naturally [says Ryle] the addicts of the superstition that all true indicative sentences either describe existents or report occurrences will demand that sentences such as " this wire conducts electricity ", or " John Doe knows French ", shall be construed as conveying factual information of the same type as that conveyed by " this wire is conducting electricity " and " John Doe is speaking French ". How could the statements be true unless there were something now going on, even though going on, unfortunately, behind the scenes? Yet they have to agree that we do often know that a wire conducts electricity and that individuals know French, without having first discovered any undiscoverable goings-on. . . . Dispositional statements are neither reports of observed or observable states of affairs, nor yet reports of unobserved or unobservable states of affairs.
>
> (*Concept*, pp. 124-5)

One is hard put to it to know who are or were the addicts of the superstition of occult goings-on behind the scenes. But dispositional statements do report states of affairs. As I have shown, to say the glass is thick is no less a dispositional statement than to say it is brittle, and to say it broke because it was brittle is a statement of the same type as to say it did not break because it was thick, or that it broke because it was thin. The dangerous condition of the factory, again, is the explosive material lying about. If that is not a state of affairs, what is? To say " this wire conducts electricity " may mean that it is commonly used for that purpose. But to say it is a good conductor is to ascribe a property to it, and this is sought in the physical constitution of the wire, and this again is a condition, a causal condition, of conduction. The condition is that it has " free " electrons: this is the nature of metals. If it were not what it is, e.g. copper, Cu, it would not conduct the current. Its being copper is the causal condition of good conduction on various occasions. But if there is any such wire, it is what it is with all its properties now. Now Ryle has given no reason for supposing that " knowing French " is less a causal condition of speaking French on various occasions than " being Cu " is a causal condition of good conduction on various occasions. Just as the properties of the wire, whereby it is what it is, are causes of its behaving as it does on various occasions and in various circumstances, so John Doe's properties would be causes of his behaving as he does in various circumstances.

This is a view which is widely held by behaviourists, some physiologists, and cyberneticists, and they are quite clear about what a causal explanation is. But Russell in *The Analysis of Mind* is as good a case in point as any. The occurrences which in Ryle's doctrine would verify the general hypothetical propositions correspond to what Russell calls mnemic phenomena, which are to be explained by mnemic causal laws. According to this account, the response of an organism to a present stimulus is very often dependent upon the past history of the organism and not merely upon the stimulus: past occurrences in addition to the present stimulus and the present ascertainable conditions of the organism enter into the causation of the response (*Analysis*, p. 77). Russell unfortunately does not make it quite clear that such an account applies not only to the behaviour of organisms but to that of inanimate things. The temper of a steel blade or the tensile strength of a girder may be regarded in the same light. When the blade cuts wood or the girder takes a strain, the present occurrence is the effect in part of the state of the steel and of the processes of manufacture. Its past history determines its present behaviour, as, to quote Russell's example, the burnt child fears the fire.

Intelligent machines: Ryle's account of dispositional properties tends to obscure what is meant by causal explanation, and he does not seem to recognise that his account of human dispositions and propensities is essentially causal by the same token as the other dispositions and propensities of things which he cites. My next criticism is closely connected with this. It is that Ryle's concept of a machine or mechanism is inadequate. At the end of his chapter on the will, he writes as follows:

> In conclusion, it is perhaps worth while giving a warning against a very popular fallacy. The hearsay knowledge that everything in Nature is subject to mechanical laws often tempts people to say that Nature is either one big machine, or else a conglomeration of machines. But in fact there are very few machines in Nature. The only machines that we find are the machines that human beings make, such as clocks, windmills and turbines. There are a very few natural systems which somewhat resemble such machines, namely, such things as solar systems. These do go on by themselves and repeat indefinitely the same series of movements. . . . Paradoxical though it may seem, we have to look rather to living organisms for examples in Nature of self-maintaining, routine-observing systems. The movements of the heavenly bodies provided one kind of clock. It was the human pulse that provided the next. Nor is it merely primitive animism which makes native children think of engines as iron horses. There is very little else in Nature to which they are so closely analogous. Avalanches and games of billiards are subject to mechanical laws; but they are not at all like the workings of machines.
>
> *(Concept*, p. 82)

On the previous page, Ryle has asserted: " Men are not machines, not even ghost-ridden machines. They are men – a tautology which is sometimes worth remembering." This is a tautology perhaps, but up to the point at which these passages occur there is more to controvert than to support Ryle's contention. If machines are defined as man-made, then indeed men are not machines. Now this indeed conforms to ordinary usage: what we call a machine is designed by men to serve some purpose. It is in fact not very easy to define a machine. If, however, there were things which were not man-made but which otherwise had the essential characteristics of certain types of machine, we should have to change our concept of a machine. But a machine, for Ryle, repeats indefinitely the same series of movements, and when he mentions living organisms as examples of " self-maintaining routine-observing systems " it appears to be in the same sense as solar systems are self-maintaining and routine-observing. But this is not the sense in which it has been claimed that organisms, including the human organism, are machines. (It was not even the sense in which Descartes suggested that other animals were automata.) Organisms are self-maintaining, given the right environment, in a much more complex way. If the concept of a biochemical mechanism be admitted, and a machine be a self-maintaining system of mechanisms, an organism can very well be regarded as a biochemical machine. The homeostatic mechanisms in the organism, which maintain it through changes of external and internal environment, function as what the communications engineers called negative feedback mechanisms.[1]

Now man-made systems incorporating such mechanisms reproduce, and are intended to reproduce, some features of human behaviour, and to improve upon it. Indeed, that is the point of them. By the observational behaviouristic criteria which Ryle applies to men, they learn, remember, correct their errors, display purpose, and act intelligently. In Ryle's chapter on 'Knowing How and Knowing That' passage after passage would apply to some of the more "sophisticated" of these machines – not in every detail, of course. Nor do they only do what they were designed to do: they can do things which their designers did not bargain for.[2] If, as Ryle says, the chessboard is among the places of the mind, the places where people work or play stupidly or intelligently, what is one to say of a chess-playing machine?

---

[1] Of all that has been written on this subject, I think the best general account is still Norbert Wiener's pioneer work *Cybernetics* (Wiley, 1948; M.I.T.).

[2] See Norbert Wiener, 'The Brain and the Machine' in *Dimensions of Mind*, ed. Sydney Hook (New York: Collier-Macmillan, 1961).

After the initial programming, it can be programmed by playing against it. Ryle's account of what constitutes good markmanship in the section entitled 'The Exercise of Intelligence' (*Concept*, p. 45) applies to the most advanced type of automatically controlled anti-aircraft gun in use by 1945. By all Ryle's criteria it was much more skilled and intelligent than any human marksman.

In his account of what happens when a person argues intelligently (*Concept*, p. 47) Ryle says: " Underlying all the other features of the operations executed by the intelligent reasoner there is the cardinal feature that he reasons logically, that is, that he avoids fallacies and produces valid proofs and inferences, pertinent to the case he is making." If this is the cardinal feature of arguing intelligently, some machines argue intelligently. Other features cited by Ryle, such as observing the rules of professional etiquette or exploiting ambiguities, they lack.

But they do innovate. The intelligent reasoner, says Ryle, " has to innovate, and where he innovates, he is not operating from habit. He is not repeating hackneyed moves." And that he is thinking what he is doing is shown in part by " this fact that he is operating without precedents ". Machines with " higher order programming " are provided with what are called assessment rules to enable them to innovate in new situations.

Ryle, it would seem, is obliged to hold that some machines think. For if they think what they are doing, as by some of Ryle's criteria they do, then of course they think. Ryle has not only provided no evidence for his statement that men are not machines, but on the contrary described human skills and abilities in a way which is compatible with that hypothesis. He plainly did not intend to do this. Nor did he intend in his account of dispositions and propensities to give a causal account of human behaviour. But it seems to me that he has.

CHAPTER NINETEEN

THE SELF AND OTHERS – I

To ask the question " what knowledge can a person get of the work-ings of his own mind? " says Ryle (*Concept*, p. 168), is to invite an absurd answer about his peeps into a windowless chamber to which only he has access. An introspectionist answer. To get the proper answer one must ask: " How do we establish law-like propositions about the overt and silent behaviour of persons? " And the answer is that we just observe, watch, notice, listen to and compare the behaviour of persons. Just, it may be asked, as we observe, watch, etc., the behaviour of rats, volcanoes or T.N.T.? Ryle gives no ground for thinking otherwise. Ryle is not indeed an ortho-dox behaviourist, for the orthodox behaviourist offers an ex-plicitly causal account of human behaviour. But he is unorthodox only in the sense that he does not realise that explanation in terms of dispositions and propensities, as he presents it, amounts to causal explanation.

> There is [says Ryle] a considerable logical hazard in using the nouns ' mind ' and ' minds ' at all . . . . Where logical candour is required from us, we ought to follow the example set by novelists, biographers and diarists, who speak only of persons doing and undergoing things.
>
> (*Concept*, p. 168)

I am a person, according to Ryle, but I can observe that person only in much the same way as I observe any other person, except that I can listen to more of *his* conversations, as I am the addressee of *his* unspoken soliloquies, and notice more of *his* excuses, as I am never absent when they are made (*Concept*, p. 169). I can ask how I find out that this person has seen a joke. I can eavesdrop on *his* utterances and discover the frames of mind which these utterances disclose (*Concept*, p. 184). I can also hold sociable interchanges of conversations with him (*Concept*, p. 185). It should, one might think, be possible for me to eavesdrop on *his* sociable interchanges with himself. To think " What fun the two of *them* are having! " or ask, " What would they say if they knew I was listening? " or even " What would *they* say if they knew *we* were listening? " Again, self-control is " simply the management of an ordinary person by an ordinary person, namely where John Doe, say, is taking both parts " (*Concept*, p. 195).

The question is: is John Doe one person or two or more? When I observe myself, or listen to the interesting things I say, or am addressed by myself, or hear "his" excuses, or eavesdrop on "his" utterances, or discover " his " frames of mind, am I one person or two or more? If two or more, how do I tell which is which? If " person " be used univocally, we are landed with a contradiction: one person is two persons, the other is the same.

How has logical candour been advanced or logical hazard avoided by talking of persons?

How does the contradiction or equivocation arise? It arises, I suggest, from the view that all knowledge is empirical, objective knowledge, knowledge of matters of fact, established by empirical observation, whether the thing observed is a piece of glass, a wire, T.N.T., or a person. Since one is a person, which is at least a human body anticking about the world, whatever is to be known about it is to be known, not only in the same way as what is to be known about any other person, but in essentially the same way as whatever is to be known of anything. It is of course a different sort of thing from rocks and trees and amœbae, but a thing nonetheless. Genuine knowledge of it is objective knowledge by the same token as knowledge of anything else. Not only is the self another other (which, in a sense to be explained, is true) but all others are objects. There are residual but unimportant differences in the supplies of data, and that is all.

The first or second person (whichever one prefers) of the two-person person is the ghost that haunts all theories which attempt to reduce the self to another object: the disembodied epistemological subject. This it is which observes, watches, notices, listens to, and compares the behaviour (including the discourse) of persons, among whom, or which, is one it calls " myself ". Apart from the fact that it is always tied to one person, and other persons will keep going away or failing to turn up, persons have learnt the trick of thinking silently instead of aloud, so that the ghost cannot always hear what they are thinking even when they are present. How does it know that they do think silently? It knows this because its own particular person uses this trick. But in this case, though the thinking is silent, the ghost hears and overhears and eavesdrops just as if its person were thinking aloud. It doesn't of course have eyes to see or ears to hear – the person has these. But ghosts do not need these to observe, watch, notice, listen or compare.

It is impossible to see how the ghost can ever be laid. Let us assume that there is no ghost, and then watch it appearing. Let us accept Ryle's account of how dispositional questions, performance questions, and occurrence questions are decided: by watching, following, noticing, listening, etc. How do I watch, follow, notice, listen, etc.? With my eyes and ears. How do I know or find out that I watch, follow, notice, listen, etc.? Since these are occurrences and per-formances, the answer has to be by watching, following, noticing, listening, etc. But not with my eyes and ears. And behold the ghost.

At a later stage, the person and his *Doppelgänger* are replaced by acts of the first, second, third and higher orders. An act can never be the subject in itself, but only of a further act of a higher order. The making of every entry in a diary may be chronicled in the diary except the last one.

> This, I think [says Ryle] explains the feeling that my last year's self, or my yesterday's self, could in principle be described and accounted for, and that your past or present self could be ex-haustively described and accounted for by me, but that my today's self perpetually slips out of any hold of it that I try to make. It also explains the apparent non-parallelism betwee the notion of " I " and that of " you ", without construing the elusive residuum as any kind of ultimate mystery.
>
> (*Concept*, p. 196)

Now I do not have this feeling about my last year's or yesterday's self, but if I did, I should still, I think, find it difficult to agree that Ryle has explained it. Let us ask in what sense one could " in principle " exhaustively describe and account for one's past conduct. There is one well-known sense in which this has been alleged to be possible in principle, and this is precisely the sense in which it has been alleged that all our future conduct is in principle predictable: the sense proposed by La Mettrie, d'Holbach, and many subsequent mechanical determinists. There is today more than one reason why people who are inclined to hold such a view in a more sophisticated form do not hold it. The simplest reason, however, is this – that no satisfactory meaning can be attached to " in principle ". What it is alleged could be done cannot be done in fact, and we cannot say how it could be done. The meaningful use of " in principle " is in cases where one has the knowledge and techniques to do something which hasn't been done, and may never be done because it is too expensive or not worth while, e.g. to produce a gas-turbine motor car. This is possible " in principle ", because we know the principle. It is pointless to say we can predict in principle what we haven't the remotest notion of how to predict.

Now the point Ryle appears to be making is that while one's past in principle can be exhaustively accounted for, one's future is unpredictable, for one datum relevant to the prediction, the prediction itself, must be left out of account. It is a higher order operation. Now again, I think Ryle masks from himself and the unwary reader the fact that what he is concerned with is causal explanation and prediction. That this is what he is about is made plain in the paragraph following the one I have quoted:

> When people consider the problems of the Freedom of the Will and try to imagine their own careers as analogous to those of clocks and water-courses, they tend to boggle at the idea that their own immediate future is already unalterably fixed and predictable. It seems absurd to suppose that what I am just about to think, feel, or do is already pre-appointed. . . .
>
> The solution is as before. A prediction of a deed or thought

is a higher order operation, the performance of which cannot be among the things considered in making the prediction. Yet as the state of mind in which I am just before I do something may make some difference to what I do, it follows that I must overlook at least one of the data relevant to my prediction. . . .

The fact that my immediate future is in this way systematically elusive to me has, of course, no tendency to prove that my career is in principle unpredictable to prophets other than myself, or even that it is inexplicable to myself after the heat of the action.

(*Concept*, pp. 196–7)

The difference between a causal explanation of what has happened and a prediction of what is going to happen is simply – if I may be forgiven for saying so – that what has happened has happened and what is predicted has not. There is no more difficulty essentially in the one than in the other; it depends upon the amount of relevant information and data. For this reason many causal predictions are highly reliable, while many causal explanations of past events are highly unreliable, the relevant data being irrecoverable. The contrary is often supposed or tacitly assumed, and the question is even carelessly posed in discussions of causality and induction: How do we know that causal laws which always held good in the past will always hold good in the future? But in fact we are neither more nor less in a position to say that they always held good in the past than that they will always hold good in the future. The future we predict is the future of the present as we know it. But we don't know all there is to know. That is why we are poor prophets. For like reasons, we are worse historians. We don't know enough.

If, then, the sense in which my last year's or yesterday's self could "in principle be exhaustively described and accounted for" is the causal sense, this is equally true or untrue of my today's or tomorrow's self.

In another sense, however, we know far more about our past than about our future, and can account for a good deal of it, though not causally and not exhaustively. We know far more about what we have done and why, than about what we are going to do. The reason is not far to seek: we haven't thought much about what we're going to do yet; and so far as we have, we have been deciding what we will do if the circumstances turn out as we expect, making up our minds, forming intentions. But we have not been making predictions except about the circumstances which we should have to face.

The account we give of our past is causal in so far as it concerns what happened to us or befell us – a soaking, a broken leg, the 'flu, a loss on the Stock Exchange, a war; whether or not we were responsible for it, that is, whether or not it was the foreseeable consequence or effect of our own actions. But a large part of the account is not about the happenings – what one had to contend with – and not causal. It is about what one did and why one did it, why one wanted to do it or decided to do it or thought one ought to do it, for what purpose, and so on. It is the same sort of account as we give of what we intend or propose to do. The account is largely concerned with one's actions and the reasons for them. Since this is not a causal account, it is difficult to see in what sense anyone can suppose that it was all pre-appointed, unless he holds the doctrine of predestination in which everything can be accounted for, but only in eternity and only by God. It is just as difficult to see in what sense one's past was pre-appointed as to see in what sense one's future can be, unless one is trying to give a causal account. But this is not the sort of account we do or can give, except as regards what happens to us or befalls us. But it is such an account that Ryle has in mind, and he makes this plain when he cites a " state of mind " as a datum relevant to a prediction, i.e. a contributory cause of subsequent conduct. Our predicting such-and-such on this view is a mental event, an effect of antecedent events, and a contributory cause of subsequent events.

But the account which we can and do give of our past is not of this kind, nor of anyone else's past, except when we want to make excuses, disclaim responsibility, or avoid blame. It is because we think we might have done otherwise than we did that we often think we've been fools, if not knaves. If we thought our past was pre-appointed, how could we?

It is therefore not very clear what problem Ryle's " solution " is a solution to, since his premise – an unconfessed premise – that we give a causal account of our own past life is false. The difficulty of predicting our own future causally would be only marginally greater than that of accounting for our own past causally – physiologically, neurologically, genetically, chemically, physically, economically, geographically, climatically, dietetically, etc. Only people who do not take causality seriously, as I do, could suppose otherwise. How could I even begin to give a causal account of my past? But I know why I did this and that: what my reasons were.

As it is a mistake to suppose that we account for our past causally, except as regards what happens to us with or without our own prior agency, so it is a mistake to suppose that we even try causally to predict our future. We can say what we intend to do – if we've thought about it – and give our reasons for doing it, say what our purpose is, and so on. But this is not to make a prediction. If we later change our minds it won't be because we have previously made up our minds. We can, if we like, make general predictions – that we shall eat on more than 99 per cent of our future days, that our intake of calories *per diem* will be above 2000 (if we are Europeans), and so on. But since we should not be able to do whatever we might want to do if some such general conditions were not fulfilled, we shall in effect take steps to see that they are fulfilled. Other questions about our future concern what we intend to do. What one predicts are the circumstances which one cannot control.

" My process of pre-envisaging may divert the course of my ensuing behaviour in a direction and degree of which my prognosis cannot take account. One thing I cannot prepare myself for is the next thought I am going to think." The last sentence is tautologous: to be conscious is to be conscious now, not somehow or other in the future, whether one is thinking *of* the past or *of* the future. But the point about pre-envisaging is to think of the future and what one should do. That is one of the points about thinking – we can think about what we might do before actually doing it. But for this, we should all be dead. But my immediate future is not systematically elusive to me, as Ryle alleges. I am bent on getting this chapter finished before lunch. The sense in which it can be said to be elusive is simply the sense in which consciousness – thinking, remembering, seeing, foreseeing, imagining, etc. – is always now. But consciousness is not an object, not a series of happenings or events. We can only project or envisage the future now; the future is the future in relation to now. The sense in which the future is elusive – a grotesque sense – is that it is not now. This truism seems to underlie much of Ryle's very obscure argument. Now I have a fair idea of what others will do (and they of what I shall do). How? I understand why they should want to do it and can't imagine why they should want to do otherwise. That is also why they sometimes surprise me. But there is no question here of prophecy or causal prediction. I explain their actions in the way I explain my own. I have little idea of what the causes are in the one case or in the other. I understand or fail to understand what they are up to in terms of my own experience as a being with purposes and desires and reasons for doing things. Some of them are said to be predictable (the bores) and some unpredictable (the nuisances) but one cannot readily think of a causal explanation of their conduct. Reliable people are people one can trust, not people one can make causal predictions about. They are people who would not deceive one or let one down. The explanation of this which we give is not causal. It is that they think it wrong to deceive or that they are devoted to one or love one. It is not that certain mental or other events or states of mind occurred in their history.

Ryle seems to confuse causal prediction with having intentions and understanding other people's intentions and conduct, and the difficulties of prediction with the perpetual presence of consciousness – the impossibility of thinking one's next thought in advance.

CHAPTER TWENTY

THE SELF AND OTHERS – II

RYLE's account of self-knowledge and his account of our knowledge of others are, I believe, open to the same criticism. Though I have made my essential points about embodied experience and reflexion, I will briefly repeat one or two of them in order to show how reflexion is enmeshed with knowledge or understanding of others.

What a person can know of his own body as an object or thing in the world empirically by observation and experiment is rather less than what he can find out about another body. But his own embodied experience – seeing, touching, moving, breathing, laughing, sneezing, being elated or depressed, talking (meaning aloud) – is not an object or thing which may be empirically observed, nor the antics of an observable thing, nor is it his observation of a body; it is his being a body. Only by being a body is he in the world and only so can he observe any body or know anything about any body. There can be no objective, empirical, scientific account of the embodied subject, for it is, *a priori*, presupposed in any such account.

But, it may be said, at least we know about others objectively, empirically, by observation, by their observed behaviour, just as we know about the brittleness of glass, the conductivity of copper wire, the explosiveness of T.N.T. This is roughly Ryle's view, his main view, though in practice he often departs from it. But the answer is " no ", not primarily. There are of course many facts to be known about people, such as their date of birth and bodily measurements, which are objectively determinable. But in accounting for and understanding their conduct, we do so, so far as we may, by virtue of knowing them as others. Others are not other things, other organisms, but other embodied subjects, seeing, feeling, projecting, trying to do this and that, with ends in view. If, and to the extent that, they are at all predictable, that is why.

Ryle could not say half the things he says in *The Concept of Mind* if this were not so. But he does not seem to realise it. And the reason, I suggest, is that he is the victim of an intellectualist legend much more insidious than those he attacks: the empiricist theory of knowledge whereby we know whatever we know by objective observation or reports of such, by experimentation and induction, and understand or explain whatever we understand or explain causally, scientifically. His restoration of self-knowledge to " approximate parity " with knowledge of others consists in the reduction of the self to another other and all others to objects of empirical investigation. There is a residual difference in the supplies of data, he says, and this reveals very clearly the type of knowledge he has in mind. It is possibly because he knows this won't do that he says such odd things about causal explanation and even goes to the extent of denying that the most evidently causal explanations are causal.

It is through our own affective consciousness of the world with all the values, apprehended as they are, there in it, that we understand the conduct of others. As Hume so well understood, the springs of action lie in the passions, and we understand what others are about because we know what it's like, what they feel, the way they see the situation. Our relation to others is not in the first place that of subject to object, of self to things, but of embodied subject or self to other embodied subjects or selves. As children even our relation to things has something of this character, and in some ways we remain animists in our relation to some things, to ships or to friendly old houses, for instance. Of course, we know they are just sticks and stones and ironmongery, but we are sad at their decay and destruction.

We see the expressions and attitudes of others and understand their meaning as we understand the meaning of their words. We see the look in their eyes, which is not to see or look at or examine an eye as a thing. We feel their eyes upon us and are affected thereby in our being as we could never be by a thing. We understand and explain their conduct, so far as we do, because we know reflexively what it is to see, hear, move, grasp, be elated or depressed, or angry or afraid or disappointed. We understand their reasons by seeing the situation they are in. And our explanations of the conduct of others in the normal way are entirely based upon this reflexive understanding. Whereas causal explanations are never final, explanations of this sort frequently are final for they answer the question " Why? " as causal explanations never do.

We are others for them, and know it when we see them look at us and when they speak to us, and we read in their expression and attitude what they feel about us. We are, in their view, approved or disapproved, dull or amusing, admired or despised, loved or disliked. The other is another self, the self another other. It is in this dialectical relation that self-knowledge and knowledge of others are inseparably intertwined. Reflexively we understand how we look in the other's eyes, we are conscious of being *en soi pour autrui*. If there is an " approximate parity " it is by virtue of this dialectic. Ryle talks freely of vanity, for example, but never of this dialectic whereby we are vain and whereby we understand the vanity of others.

Ryle makes much of such things as tones of voice, whose meaning could only be understood as the expression of another embodied subject and not as a mere sound. And in his treatment of avowals and unstudied utterances, surely a most promising tack, he in effect misses the essential point by making all selves others and only others, so that we hear our own unstudied utterances exactly in the same way as we hear others' unstudied utterances, which is to say " we " do not utter, do not say, do not mean aloud. " We " know we are depressed or elated by hearing our own words, not by being depressed or elated, not reflexively, but empirically by observation of our curious behaviour. " We ", as I have said, in this context can only be the ghost, the disembodied epistemological subject.

For reasons I have expounded before, others may know our mood or feeling before we do, but our words or tone are not *sui generis* and not mere happenings or events, their meaning is our meaning, our expression. Our explicit avowals of feelings, moods and emotions are already reflexive and express our reflexive awareness. Of course Ryle knows this. How could anyone discuss " catching oneself beginning to dream " without knowing it? But Ryle is so concerned to make knowledge of the self and others objective and matter-of-fact, to get rid of the ghost and its analogical inference to other ghosts, that he makes us all indeed others, but not selves, and this is to make all of us, all so-called others, things. The only explanation of the behaviour of things is a causal explanation. Apart from this, how should the so-called problem of predicting one's own future behaviour or indeed one's own thoughts ever arise? Surely no one who has not been bamboozled by pseudo-science ever tries to do this; what he tries to predict is the circumstances he will have to contend with; in making up his mind what to do he is not predicting what he will do, but deciding what he had better do.

CHAPTER TWENTY-ONE

LOGICAL GRAMMAR
AND REFLEXION

RYLE is engaged, and heavily engaged, in reflexive description at various points throughout the book. But he does not or will not recognise it, nor pursue it systematically. His account of what he is doing is that he is trying to "show why certain sorts of operations with the concepts of mental powers and processes are breaches of logical rules" (*Concept*, p. 8). One might not guess from his account of what he is doing that his discussion of the "logical rules" or "logical grammar" of words is a discussion of what we embodied subjects mean by what we say. One might suppose that the logical rules and grammar of the language as he *professes* to discuss them were matters for the grammarian, the philologist, and the lexicographer, and though Ryle is rightly convinced that he is doing something different from any of them, he never quite explains what it is, nor where the difference lies (' La Philosophie analytique ', p. 100).

It is in one of his best chapters, ' Sensation and Observation ', that he says:

> There is something seriously amiss with the discussions occupying this chapter. I have talked as if we know how to use the concept or concepts of sensation; I have spoken with almost perfunctory regret of our lack of ' neat ' sensation words; and I have glibly spoken of auditory and visual sensations. But I am sure that none of this will do.
>
> (*Concept*, p. 240)

Ryle in fact uses the ambiguous vocabulary of sensations but recognises that is a semi-psychological, semi-physiological term, the

188

employment of which is allied with certain pseudo-scientific, Cartesian theories, and he confesses that he does not know the "right idioms" in which to discuss these matters. Even in the process of using the vocabulary and falling into some of the errors, he succeeds in seeing that it won't do. But he seems to be making the odd suggestion that there *are* "right idioms" which he, a highly articulate man, does not know; as if the language were *sui generis*, as if it had some existence independent of those who speak it, as if its meanings and idioms were not our meanings and idioms, and as if we were stumped if we could not find one ready-made.

"We do not", he says, "and cannot describe haystacks in terms of this and that set of sensations. We describe our sensations by certain sorts of references to observers and things like haystacks." (*Concept*, p. 203.) The sensations Ryle is talking about are not, for example, the pricking of the hay when one leans against a haystack. But what other sensations are there? He later remarks (*Concept*, p. 203) that sensations do not have sizes, shapes, positions, temperatures, colours or smells. This is not quite true of bodily sensations – a pain in the toe is in the toe and in this sense has position, and similarly some pains are in a small area and some spread, e.g. all up and down the leg. But the question is: what sensations can we describe and what sensations are there, apart from bodily sensations? It is true of bodily sensations that one does not and cannot observe them, as Ryle points out, though one can attend to them, for example, to the feel of one's collar on the back of the neck. But Ryle insists:

> To describe someone as finding a thimble is to say something about his having visual, tactual or auditory sensations, but it is to say more than that. Similarly to describe someone as trying to make out whether what he sees is a chaffinch or a robin, or a stick or a shadow, a fly on the window or a mote in his eye, is to say something about his visual sensations, but it is to say more than that.
>
> (*Concept*, p. 224)

It is surely not to say that at all. To try to make out what one sees is to try to make out what it is. What is the point of calling the indeterminate " it " a sensation? But what else could one be calling a sensation? And what could one be saying about it? The same point arises at the end of his good description of the experience of recognising a tune and listening to a familiar tune. Ryle says that when we hear a tune we are having auditory sensations, but more than that. But what could they be but the notes of the tune we hear? And why call them sensations? There is always a distinction to be made between the " this " and the " such ", but " this ", is always " such-and-such ", the universal is *in re*, the tune we hear – for example, " Lillibullero ", though we may not know the name – is this tune now.

Now it is possible that what Ryle is after is the various aspects of things, the fact that a thing is never seen in its entirety all at once, that it must be explored, gone round, discovered and learned. " Sensations " would refer to visible parts of the haystack as distinct from the other side or the inside. But if this is the point, it is not made clear, and the term " sensation " merely leads to confusion.

On p. 206, Ryle says: " We have seen that observing entails having sensations; a man could not be described as watching a robin who had not got a single glimpse of it, or as smelling cheese who had not caught a whiff. (I am pretending, what is not true, that words like ' glimpse ' and ' whiff' stand for sensations. . . .) " He goes on to show the absurdity of supposing that we observe the glimpse. But why should he pretend that glimpses are sensations? To catch a glimpse of a robin is to see a robin for a brief moment before it disappears from view. To watch a robin is not to be catching glimpses of it unless it is popping into and out of view. But the glimpsing or catching glimpses is the seeing. The whiff on the other hand is not the smelling but what is smelt. Smells are smelt with the nose, not in the nose, but in the air, in the room. To get a whiff of cheese is to smell briefly the smell of cheese, coming, for example, from the grocer's door as one passes. (If smells were *in* the nose, they would not come from any direction: other animals of course find their prey by smell or take flight from their enemies in the direction away from the smell.) There is no more reason to call smells or whiffs sensations than to call the brown of the table-top a sensation.

At the end of the chapter, where he is discussing hurts and itches, Ryle says:

> Hurts and itches cannot, for instance, be distinct or indistinct, clear or unclear. Whereas finding something out by sight or touch is an achievement, 'I itch terribly' does not report an achievement, or describe anything ascertained. I do not know what more is to be said about the logical grammar of such words, save that there is much more to be said.
>
> (*Concept*, p. 244)

What is unsatisfactory? What won't do? What more is to be said?

Ryle seems to suppose that his remaining perplexities concern the right idioms and the logical grammar of the language. But how can a man in perfect command of the language say such a thing? The genuine perplexity concerns the nature of sense-experience; there is of course a difficulty in saying precisely and unambiguously what we mean, but the primary difficulty is that of reflexive analysis of our experience. And a large part of Ryle's book consists of such analysis – never pushed very far, but unquestionably that sort of analysis, and his linguistic analyses themselves depend for understanding on the reflexive *prise de conscience* of the reader. The appeal is to the reader's experience. The reader understands him and agrees or disagrees by virtue of his own embodied being, whereby he knows what it is to see, hear, think, talk, feel, have pains and tickles, etc., in a variety of situations, and by being in possession of a language in which he means, voices and expresses his meaning, and hears with his ears others' meanings.

Why does Ryle not recognise this? Why does he repeatedly talk as if, on the one hand, the logical grammar of the language were *sui generis*, and on the other, as if whatever could be truly said of people and their conduct must be empirically, objectively, true or false, as it is true to say of a piece of wax that it is malleable, melts on heating and changes colour, and that one finds this out experimentally, inductively, by observation?

One reason is, of course, his polemical purpose of attacking dualist doctrines of mind and body, and in particular the notion of a mind as a place where things secretly happen. He identifies the contrary view chiefly with introspection, on which he launches a very effective attack, but an attack which consists essentially of asking the reader: do you have such experiences as you ought to have, if what introspectionists say is true? This is the point, and not the diversity of idioms and metaphors, live and dead, in which we talk about our experience. Any such appeal is an appeal to our reflexive awareness. And this is the appeal which must be made in the case of sensations. For example, when you see a haystack what sensations do you have and where? There is no difficulty in knowing how to talk, apart from the difficulty of reflexive analysis. It is reflexive analysis that can be difficult.

For example, if one comes out of a cool dark room into brilliant hot sunshine, how is the glare experienced? One sees the glaring colour of things, but also one cannot bear it – it hurts the eyes, one has to screw them up, and they water. One is having sensations in the eyes as well as seeing the glare of the colours, but the glare is not the discomfort in the eye; it is what hurts them. (In other conditions what one sees isn't producing any feeling in the eye.) The hurt subsides with the glare that hurts; from being glaring the colours become brilliant. One can look at them now. One does not look at the glare. If one asks if glare is a sensation, one won't get an illuminating answer, because if anything this is a matter of linguistic legislation – one must just say what reflexion reveals. Now why on earth should our experience of glare be like, much less exactly like, any other experience or described in a sensation vocabulary? It is of course analogous to other experiences. For example, one feels the hot, hard, metal pot-handle as one sees the colours of the flowers, but it is too hot to take hold of, just as the colours are too glaring to look at. It burns; the colours glare.

But to try to find a *proper* sensation vocabulary is futile. If we thought we had found one, it would merely stop us from saying half the things we want to say,[1] and still worse lead us into the pitfall of

[1] This is why some North American psychologists cannot say anything in a simple straightforward way.

the old sensationalist doctrine which has to insist that we don't experience what we think, or fondly imagine, we experience. The hankering for a " neat vocabulary " in the interests of logical grammar is fortunately doomed to disappointment. Language never fails us if we have something to say. One only lacks words when one hasn't yet got anything to say. One can go on correcting, adjusting, varying the expression, but this, as Ryle in effect says, is not something independent of thinking the matter out. To do that *is* to think the matter out. There is no problem of the idioms as such; if there were " right idioms " which Ryle didn't know, this would mean simply that someone had thought the matter out before, but Ryle hadn't read what he had to say. Idioms are not *sui generis*. There was a first time for every idiom and metaphor in the language – someone invented it, expressed his meaning that way, and his meaning was his thinking.

Ryle's discussion of consciousness is a witty survey of some of the many senses the word has in English. But the only philosophical point of this would be to guard against misunderstanding in saying what one had to say about consciousness, in whatever sense of the word one wanted to say something about it. Otherwise one is talking about the peculiar idioms of the English language, in much the same way as Otto Jespersen and other philologists. It has no relevance to the interesting and illuminating things Sartre, for example, has to say about the imaging consciousness in *L'Imaginaire*. Ryle's belief that philosophical perplexity is a matter of not knowing the right idioms or of not having got them sorted out – as if they were all there, somewhere, if one could find them, ready-made – accounts for his failure to consider reflexive awareness or consciousness on which all descriptions of experience depend and to which he constantly appeals.

He takes what is " apt to be inadequately covered by the umbrella-title ' self-consciousness ' " to be higher order acts of various sorts, of which reviews of books, criticism of actions, and so on are the types. But reflexion is not a higher order act of this kind, nor is there any sort of public or private performance to be the object of it. It is not observation, and it has no object analogous to the book which is criticised or the scoring of the goal which is praised. The object is the object of experience in the ordinary sense – the tree that one sees, for instance. An experience becomes reflexive: reflexion makes explicit what is implicit in it, it is the *prise de conscience*, not the observation of another object. There is nothing obscure or occult about it. Without it, no one could appeal to anyone else's experience; novels would be incomprehensible, and the *moraliste's aperçus* on the human heart could never be found penetrating.

No experience need become reflexive, though many experiences do. Reflexive analysis is always possible. To be reflexively aware of seeing one must be seeing. To be reflexively aware of writing one must be writing. Most of the time one isn't reflexively aware of writing. But one can be. If one asks what is the difference between writing oneself, seeing the pen and paper, and seeing someone else writing, the answer is given by reflexion. For example, as one writes one does not watch to see what letter or word comes next, nor does one even watch the tip of the pen forming the letters; one writes the word as a whole in cursive, not as a series of letters, but one may notice when one hasn't formed a letter properly or when one has misspelt a word. In looking at what someone else is writing, one watches the letters appearing and guesses from the context and the beginning of the word what the word will be. Reflexive analysis here merely makes explicit a difference of which everyone is more or less aware. There is of course an analogy with the difference between saying something and hearing someone else say something. (As I have remarked earlier, one might suppose from what Ryle says that it was merely a matter of the different mouths the sounds came out of and the position of various pairs of ears in relation to these mouths.)

Reflexion may be retrospective and is presupposed in memory of having seen and heard and done such-and-such. To remember the name of the capital of Colombia when asked does not involve reflexion – but to " know " that one knows it and *try* to remember it, or to " know " that one doesn't, are reflexive, and so of course is remembering having seen it mentioned in the newspaper yesterday, whether or not one also remembers the name. The reflexive description and analysis of the experience of " knowing one knows but not being able to recall " is a matter of some difficulty, but without reflexive awareness – not empirical observation – no one would even know what I was talking about when I mention it. According to Ryle's official account we could only know this by hearing another person – whether or not it happened to be ourself – saying, "Oh, I *know* it but it's slipped my memory", by overhearing his unstudied utterances. And according to Ryle, he *wouldn't* know it since he couldn't say it.

When one asks what the difference is between a happening, event or occurrence, and an action or deed, or what the difference is between something moving, or a movement taking place, and a movement that one makes, if people are at a loss it is not because they doubt the difference or because the difference is obscure, but because it is already familiar reflexively and is already expressed in the very words in which the question is asked. Everyone knows the difference between something happening to him and his doing something; everyone has experienced the effects of external agencies and everyone is a doer with desires and ends in view which he sets about achieving. It is upon this common reflexive understanding that the analysis of experience, including the analysis of meaning, is founded. That Ryle's analysis of concepts is founded upon it and presupposes it is readily shown.

Take, for example, his statement: "Hurts and itches cannot, for instance, be distinct or indistinct, clear or unclear." They can be mild or dull, or severe or acute. How do we assent to, or dissent from this? By thinking of hurts and itches, for we know what various sorts of hurts and itches are like reflexively, what it is to have a hurt or an itch, as we know what it is like to see something clearly, to make it out, and to see something indistinctly, for example in a bad light. To think of, in such cases, is to imagine having an itch, seeing a haystack through a fog, etc. The logical grammar of the words could only be understood by one who could be hurt or have an itch, and who was in possession of a language to express or describe these experiences.

But if one wants to dissent from Ryle's analysis of the logical grammar of these words it is easy to do so. All one has to do is to think of a kind of hurt or itch of which the word "distinct" or "indistinct" could be used, for language is essentially to be exploited. Is a fierce itch a hurt? Is an agonising burning itch, with fever, from sunburn, a hurt? Is it distinctly an itch or distinctly a hurt? Could one not call the acute but generalised discomfort of a fever when one wakes up, indistinct? That is surely why one *wonders* what it is one feels: one is distressed, but how and where? To pursue the sort of questions which Ryle raises, it is of little use to examine the English language which all we embodied English-speaking subjects know; one must think of various experiences. It worries Ryle that there is no neat sensation vocabulary. I suspect that underlying this worry is the desire for " unambiguous " words. But words are neither ambiguous nor unambiguous, only what people mean.

CHAPTER TWENTY-TWO

IMAGINATION AND EMOTION

LET us now look at Ryle's account of mental images and pictures in the mind's eye, which he has himself recognised to be akin in some respects to Sartre's reflexive analysis ('La Philosophie analytique', p. 81). It is one of his best chapters because he does so much more than he professes to be doing; the trouble is that he does not do enough of it. His refusal to pursue reflexive analysis or to concern himself with any kind of meaning but the meaning, sense or nonsense, of expressions (cf. 'Philosophie', p. 97), accounts for his failure to say some of the most obvious and central things about imagination. The result of failure to pursue the analysis of this central function of consciousness – which Hume essentially recognised – is an extreme ambiguity in some of the things he does say. This ambiguity, as I shall show, actually results from his preoccupation with words, when he ought to be analysing experience. It isn't the fault of the idioms!

> I want to show [he says] that the concept of picturing, visual-ising, or 'seeing' is a proper and useful concept, but that its use does not entail the existence of pictures which we contemplate or the existence of a gallery in which such pictures are ephemer-ally suspended. Roughly, imaging occurs, but images are not seen. . . . A person picturing his nursery . . . is not being a spectator of a resemblance of his nursery, but he is resembling a spectator of his nursery.
>
> (*Concept*, pp. 247–8)

This is fine for a start, but only for a start: images are not pictures, nor resemblances, nor representations, and they cannot be seen or looked at. But for the same reason a person imaging his nursery is *not* resembling a spectator of his nursery. A spectator of the nursery would be in it and see it and could examine all the details of it, discovering them there. For the same reason that an image is not, and cannot be, a resemblance of a nursery, a person imagining a nursery is not, and cannot be, a resemblance of a spectator of the nursery. Ryle is led, one might think quite innocently and harmlessly, into saying that he does resemble a spectator of the nursery, because he fails to make the simple, essential point about the object of the image or imagining, and the object of the seeing. It is the same object – the nursery – but imaging is not seeing. The person picturing his nursery is not in it and does not see it. But it is his nursery he is picturing. The reason why he is precisely *not* resembling a spectator is that a spectator is spectating, seeing.

An image is an imaging, a consciousness of, a mode of intending or meaning an object. As Sartre says: When I imagine my friend Peter, it is Peter I am imagining ; when I have an image of Peter, it is Peter himself that I mean. This is tautologous, even if one has no idea where Peter at present is, or what he is doing. Who or what is Peter? He is the man I mean. To image or imagine him is to mean or intend that very man in person. An old man picturing his nursery would mean or intend that very nursery in the house where he was born, then and there, three score years and ten ago, even if it were long since demolished and even if he knew it was long since demolished.

The suggestion that he is resembling a spectator of his nursery is closely connected with Ryle's tendency to regard imaging and imagining as a kind of make-believe (which of course depends upon imagining) or pretending, and his failure to realise that to think of or remember, for example, the splendid proportions of St Paul's is to imagine St Paul's, and that whenever one thinks of any actual place or person or thing in the world and remembers what he or she or it was like, one is imagining that place or person or thing. But not pretending or making-believe or fancying that. One can also imagine what one doesn't remember or believe to exist or to have existed. The point of Hume's natural belief is to make the distinction – the objects of natural belief are what we should say there is, or was, really in the world, not *figments* of the imagination, such as dragons and centaurs or Hamlet.

What Hume tries to account for by his doctrine of natural belief, whereby there is for us what we call a real world, Sartre analyses in terms of the way the imaging consciousness posits its object. The object can be posited in four ways – as non-existent, as absent, as existing elsewhere, or as " neutral " (in which case the object is not posited as existent). " These positional acts ", says Sartre, " are not added to the image once it is constituted: the positional act is constitutive of the imaging consciousness. Any other theory, in fact, besides being contrary to the data of reflexion, lands us again in the illusion of immanence." (*L'Imaginaire*, p. 24)

> When I fancy I am hearing a very loud noise [says Ryle] I am not really hearing either a loud or a faint noise: I am not having a mild auditory sensation, as I am not having an auditory sensation at all, though I am fancying that I am having an intense one. An imagined shriek is not ear-splitting, not yet is it a soothing murmur, and an imagined shriek is neither louder nor fainter than a heard murmur. It neither drowns it nor is drowned by it.
>
> (*Concept*, p. 250)

What Ryle means is plainly this: we know what it is to hear an ear-splitting shriek, but we can here and now imagine one, unruffled, unshaken, and in perfect composure, for we are not now hearing it. But it is confusing to say " when I fancy I am hearing ". To fancy one hears a shriek, or to fancy one heard the door-bell, is to think that one did hear it, but not to be sure that it was a shriek or the door-bell, or whether indeed one heard anything. To imagine a very loud noise is not to fancy or imagine one is hearing it now. Similarly to imagine one sees a man crouching at the side of a road on a dark night, when it is only a bush, is simply to see the bush as a man crouching, to take it for a man : not to imagine either a bush or a man, but to see what is in fact a bush as a man, as one might take an attendant at Madame Tussaud's for one of the exhibits and say : " I fancied I was seeing one of the waxworks." To imagine is not to fancy *that*, or imagine *that* in this sense, or to fancy that one sees or hears, or that one is having an intense auditory sensation (whatever that would be). One knows perfectly well one is not seeing or hearing ; in seeing and hearing the object is posited as present and now existent ; in imaging the object is posited as not existent, or not here, or existing elsewhere or " neutral " – the positional act is in every case negative.

There is another sense, however, in which we imagine that such-and-such is the case, the sense in which we envisage a situation and imagine people we know in it. For example, one can try to imagine what an interview will be like and what sort of questions will be asked, or one can try to imagine how a friend in some situation is bearing up. One does not suppose for a moment that one is now there ; one is not hallucinating or dreaming, though imagining may be very *vivid*. Vividness is a matter of affectivity : feelings and emotions, the states of the embodied subject correlative to the value predicates of the object, can be as strong, lively, or " real " in the absence as in the presence of the object. It is this which leads people to say : " It's as if I were there ", or " I can just *see* it! "

Ryle goes on making this confusion, or at least failing to make the distinction, between two senses of " imagining that ", and of course his use of the word " fancy " does not help. (This is connected with his tendency to assimilate imagining to make-believe.) It leads him to say that to have " a mental picture of Helvellyn " is " to imagine that we see Helvellyn in front of our noses ". To imagine here in Edinburgh, Helvellyn in Cumberland is not to imagine Helvellyn in front of this nose here in Edinburgh. It is to imagine oneself (nose and all) there looking at Helvellyn : to imagine oneself in a situation in which one is not, for one is imagining here, not there, and one's nose is here, not there.

There is a further, and important point, which is worth making in this connection: perceiving and imagining may alternate but cannot fuse or combine. (One is inclined to say they can in the case of the bush seen as a crouching footpad on the dark road, because again the fear and apprehension are as strong and lively as if it were a footpad. But in fact one sees something in the shape of a man, and this case is entirely assimilable to other mistakes of perception.) If one imagines a friend sitting, talking and laughing in the chair across this present room, to imagine him in the chair one must imagine the chair *and all*, and must cease to see it. For to see the chair is to see the backrest and seat of the chair, which one could not see if he were in it. Or is " he " transparent? Is one imagining him as transparent or as his solid, opaque self?

Let us return to the imagined shriek. Ryle has missed an essential point about this ear-splitting shriek. It is that if one imagines an ear-splitting shriek, it is an ear-splitting shriek one is imagining. To say an imagined shriek is not ear-splitting is entirely misleading. The point is simply that one is not hearing it, not that it is not ear-splitting, nor that it is not a shriek. One will never get this kind of point through the study of logical grammar – one has to imagine ear-splitting shrieks. If I now imagine the ear-splitting shriek that the secretary let out when she saw the mouse, it is that very ear-splitting shriek I imagine – I mean that very shriek, the same shriek, which I then heard but now imagine. There are not two shrieks, one heard and one imagined, but one, just as there is one girl who let out the shriek, whether seen and heard or imagined.

After saying an imagined shriek is neither ear-splitting nor a soothing murmur, Ryle continues:

> Similarly, there are not two species of murderers, those who murder people, and those who act the parts of murderers on the stage; for these last are not murderers at all. . . . As mock-murders are not murders, so imagined sights and sounds are not sights and sounds. They are not, therefore, dim sights, or faint sounds. And they are not private sights or sounds either. There is no answer to the spurious question, ' Where have you deposited the victim of your mock-murder? ' since there was no victim. There is no answer to the spurious question, ' Where do the objects reside that we fancy we see? ' since there are no such objects.
>
> (*Concept*, pp. 250–1)

Again Ryle's use of the expression " fancy we see " confuses the issue. I take him to mean " imagine ". Now there is a straight and simple answer to many questions of the kind: where is the object I am imagining? If I am imagining St Paul's, the answer is: in the

City of London, not far from the Bank, etc. That's where, because I mean that very pile in that very place, and posit it, as Sartre would say, as there existing. Again, when I recall in imagination my conversation with someone yesterday, what he said, and how he said it, the expression on his face, his laugh, his tone of voice, it is those I am now imagining. If these be called sights and sounds, I saw and heard them yesterday, and today I am recalling them in imagination, imagining them, the same sights and sounds. It is quite false that the imagined sights and sounds are not sights and sounds – they are the same sight and sounds I saw and heard. They are not now occurring and do not now " reside " anywhere – they are past. But it is them I remember and imagine now, the same ones I then saw and heard. I do not now fancy I see and hear them now, I now remember seeing and hearing them *then*. There is no analogy of the sounds and sights I now imagine with mock-murders. (Stage murders, performances of fictions, imitations, mimicry demand a separate analysis, and so do portraits and caricatures or indeed faces in the fire: the imagining consciousness is essential in all of these as Sartre has shown.) (*L'Imaginaire*, ii, ' La Famille de L'Image ', pp. 30–76.)

In his discussion of the question, " How can a person seem to hear a tune running in his head unless there is a tune to hear? " (*Concept*, p. 251), Ryle is again ambiguous. It is impossible to say whether by " seeming to hear a tune " he means " having a tune in one's head ", or " thinking one *does* hear a tune ".

> We already know [he says], and have known since childhood, in what situations to describe people as imagining that they see or hear or do things. The problem, so far as it is one, is to construe these descriptions without falling back into the idioms in which we talk of seeing horse-races, hearing concerts, and committing murders. It is into these idioms that we fall back the moment we say that to fancy one sees a dragon is to see a real dragon-phantasm, or that to pretend to commit a murder is to commit a real mock-murder, or that to seem to hear a tune is to hear a real mental tune. To adopt such linguistic practices is to try to convert into species-concepts concepts which are designed,

anyhow partly, to act as factual disclaimers. . . . Similarly a person
who ' sees Helvellyn in his mind's eye ' is not seeing either the
mountain, or a likeness of the mountain. . . .

(Concept, pp. 251–2)

Apart from Ryle's ambiguity of expression, which results from the
refusal to analyse different experiences, unlike things are here yoked
by violence together: tunes and dragons and Helvellyn. Now if one
imagines Helvellyn, it is that very mountain one imagines, a real
mountain. The factual disclaimer, if it can be called that, is that it is
there and *not* here in Edinburgh: it is posited as existing elsewhere,
in Sartre's terms. Dragons on the other hand are posited as non-
existent. There are no dragons. They are what are called fictions or
purely imaginary. Since "dragon" does not mean the same as
"gryphon" or "centaur", it is convenient to regard them as universals *in verbo* but not *in re*. Everyone knows what the word "dragon"
means, but there are no instances. What is represented in pictures of
St George and the dragon is what an instance would be like if there
were an instance, and that is also what one imagines when one imagines
a dragon. But there is no instance.

Tunes or symphonies or poems have this in common, that they are
not just real things in the world in the sense in which Helvellyn is.
They are meant identities, but ideal, that is to say they are universals.
To discuss Brahms's Fourth Symphony as such is to discuss the universal, the work itself. To discuss the performance of it last night is to
discuss a good or mediocre instance of it, how well the universal was
realised. Tunes and symphonies are instantiated every time they are
played. (But dragons are not instantiated every time they are por-
trayed: if they were instantiated they would be instantiated as animals,
not as pictures.) It does not much matter in what terms one makes
these distinctions, so long as one makes them.

In hearing a symphony or a movement of a symphony, as in all
sense experience, one hears the universal *in re*. If one has heard it
before, it is the very same symphony one hears again, *in re* both
times, then and now. A point which Ryle obscures is that *the* tune
" Lillibullero ", for example, is ideal, a universal, but *the* mountain

Helvellyn is not ideal, not a universal, but a real mountain. A performance of " Lillibullero " is heard in the world in a place, as Helvellyn is seen in a place, but the Helvellyn one sees isn't a performance or an instance of Helvellyn. It is Helvellyn itself. When one imagines Helvellyn it is that mountain in Cumberland now one is imagining. Similarly if one recalls in imagination a performance of a piece it is that very performance one is imagining. But to have a tune running in one's head or hum it aloud, is not to imagine any performance, much less to fancy one is hearing it. It is to think of, mean, intend, the tune itself, the universal.

Similarly, in the case of a poem. In the poem the value is in the words and lines themselves, not in what they are about, or not mainly in what they are about. Poetry is in this like, but not quite like music, for music as such is not about anything. To recall a poem or a piece of music is to recall an affective essence, and its *raison d'être*, so to speak, is nothing but this value or affective essence. That is why the tune or poem is not posited as existing elsewhere or as non-existent, and is not posited in Sartre's sense at all. One can have the very essence " in one's head " and find a performance by contrast a revelation or a bitter disappointment.

It is in this respect that tunes are like people one knows, who in other respects, though smaller and mobile, are like Helvellyn in being bits of stuff in the world. At a pinch one can discuss " seeing Helvellyn in the mind's eye " without bringing in affectivity and value – though to discuss imagining it *vividly*, one must – but one cannot discuss imagining one's sweetheart or mama without doing so, and one cannot discuss repeating a poem or going over a piece of music to oneself without doing so. It is affectivity which makes one say " It's as if I were there ", or " I can hear it now ", or " I can just see the darling girl ", when one knows very well it isn't and one can't. That indeed is why one is longing or wishing one could.

Tunes are noble, sad, grand, gay, jaunty, wistful, melting, insinuating, etc. As one listens one is rapt, sad, jaunty, gay, melted, entranced, etc. The distinction between hearing or seeing and imagining has no parallel in the domain of affectivity and value. This is not to say one feels the same in the presence and in the absence of a person.

On the contrary. But feelings are always present feelings here and now. One may enjoy a work far more in one's head, so to speak, than in the concert hall. There is no distinction between the emotions one is having and the emotions one is imagining having, as there is a distinction between hearing and " auralising " (cf. visualising) a tune, or between having a dear person with one and imagining him in his absence. Emotions, feelings, affectivity are equally " real " or " unreal " in either case, though to some extent of course they are different feelings – for instance, one doesn't long for someone who is present, only for someone who is absent. But when one imagines a person or a place of which one is fond, and especially if one imagines being there with him, it is like being there in the sense that one has actual feelings about it and they are not imagined feelings. Perhaps, but only perhaps, this is what Ryle is referring to sometimes when he identifies imagining something with fancying one sees it. To imagine anything vividly is to be strongly affected (see Chapter 9). To imagine its charm, grace, and other value predicates. It is not to remember the details of it – one can remember the expression or physiognomy of a face vividly without, for example, being able to remember the colour of the eyes or other details. This is not to make-believe any more than to recite a poem to oneself or go over a tune in one's head is to make-believe. One isn't pretending anything is the case which isn't the case.

Now I do not claim to have done more than make a few points about imagination. My purpose is to show the inadequacy of Ryle's approach and to demonstrate the limitations of the analysis of logical grammar. Ryle's chapters on emotion and imagination are almost completely unconnected, because he did not think that the analysis of actual experience was his, or perhaps any philosopher's, business. But he cannot avoid appealing to experience, which is to appeal to the reflexive consciousness, and giving reflexive descriptions.

At the Colloque de Royaumont on analytic philosophy in 1961, Ryle made some interesting comments on his treatment of imagination.

> I was, I think, on the right track [he says] in assimilating the notion of imagining, for example to evoke in an image, to the much more general notion of pretending, of which I understood

quite clearly other kinds such as the notions of playing and simulating. But when I came to consider imagining as a " pretending to see "[1], I felt a conceptual uneasiness, which is always a sure sign that something has gone wrong. Part of this uneasiness came from the fact that when I had previously treated visual perception proper, I got stuck over the relation between the concept of seeing, let us say, trees and stars, and that of having an optical sensory impression. This shows how conceptual investigations can't be enclosed in watertight compartments. During the long period when I was floundering, I was, however, guided by an idea which I still think is capital in the concept of imagining. It is this. A person can hear at a concert a piece he does not know, so that he at once tries to learn how the melody goes, but a person who goes over the tune in his head, must have already learned, and not have forgotten, how the tune goes: furthermore, not only must he already know how the tune goes, but he must at this instant be *using* this knowledge; he must be in fact *thinking* how the tune goes; he must be thinking how it goes, without its being played and without humming it. He must think how it goes, in its *absence*.

('La Philosophie analytique', pp. 81–2)

Would Ryle say this of a poem? In what sense could a poem be absent? Ryle, who has pointed out that one may think aloud or think silently and that there is no great difference except that aloud one communicates one's thought to other people, might have realised that there is similarly no great difference between going over a tune in one's head and humming it, or between reciting a poem silently and aloud. They aren't things that exist in the world, like Helvellyn, though they are performed – performances take place and are heard. Only a performance could be absent or " ago " – not the tune itself: if one has got it in one's head, one has got *it*.

But what stopped me [Ryle goes on] was that I didn't know what more to say on this notion of *thinking how the tune goes*. For

---

[1] *Faire semblant de voir*: this may be " fancying one sees ". The text is in French.

a man can say, even with an air of surprise, " It was almost as if I really heard the notes ". The kind of " thinking " in which he was engaged was so lively, and had such a degree of resemblance with the real thing (*avec la vie*), that it led him to compare the notes which he had simply thought to heard notes, with, however, this crucial difference that the notes in thought were only notes in thought, but were not heard at all. He did not hear a note; but he " heard " them vividly. He was, without hearing them, so alert (*éveillé*) to the sound they would have had if he had heard them, that it was almost as if they had sounded in his ears. It is because of this concept of quasi-sensory vivacity of auditorily imagined notes, among other things, that I was sure of not having succeeded in finding my way.

(' La Philosophie analytique ', p. 82)

Hume was concerned with this very problem and it seems to me, the reason or one of the reasons why he wanted to distinguish impressions and ideas simply in terms of force and vivacity was that he regarded the passions as impressions, and in the case of the passions the distinction by force and vivacity is plausible. He says in Book II than an idea of a passion can be enlivened into the passion itself, and of course his mechanism of sympathy, whereby we know what others feel, depends upon this. Now whereas it is not true that to imagine something vividly is to see it, and his distinction in terms of force and vivacity won't work there, it works very well as regards the passions. To imagine an infuriating situation that arose yesterday is actually to be angry all over again, not just to remember one was angry. That is why it all comes back so vividly before one. One remembers everyone and everything with all the value predicates. To remember the situation and remember being angry is just to have the " idea of the passion ", but it is easy for the idea to be enlivened into the passion itself, i.e. one can be quite furious again here and now. The trouble is that Hume also wants the " idea of the passion " to serve in effect as the meaning of the word, for example, the meaning of the word " anger ". As a fainter copy of the passion itself, the idea of anger isn't what someone writing a chapter on anger has in mind as he writes – if he did, he would be, ever so slightly, angry. He knows the meaning of " anger ", has the concept and is using it, but he isn't angry at all.

The explanation of the " quasi-sensory vivacity " of the remembered tune, the " auditorily imagined notes ", lies in the affective state of the embodied subject, his delight in the tune – the correlate of its gaiety or charm or other value predicate. But Ryle's chapter on the emotions is entirely unrelated to his chapter on the imagination. Hume with his rather more capacious conception of the philosopher's business made the essential connection.

BIBLIOGRAPHY

Works discussed :

Hume, David, *A Treatise of Human Nature* (ed. Sir L. A. Selby-Bigge), 2nd ed. Oxford, Clarendon Press, 1897.

Hume, David, *Enquiries concerning Human Understanding* (ed. Sir L. A. Selby-Bigge). 2nd ed. Oxford, Clarendon Press, 1962.

Russell, Bertrand, *The Analysis of Mind.* Allen & Unwin, 1921.

Ayer, A. J., *The Foundations of Empirical Knowledge.* Macmillan, 1940.

Goodman, Nelson, *The Structure of Appearance.* Harvard U.P. and Oxford, 1951.

Ryle, Gilbert, *The Concept of Mind.* Hutchinson, 1949.

Ryle, Gilbert, ' La Philosophie analytique ', *Cahiers de Royaumont, Philosophie,* no. iv. Paris, Éditions de Minuit, 1961.

Works referred to :

Austin, J. L., *Sense and Sensibilia.* London, O.U.P., 1962.

Carnap, R., *Die logische Aufbau der Welt.* Hamburg, Felix Meiner, 1961.

Cornford, F. M., *Plato's Theory of Knowledge.* London, Routledge & Kegan Paul, 1935.

Husserl, Edmund, *Logische Untersuchungen.* Halle, Max Niemeyer Verlag, 1913.

Husserliana (general ed. L. van Breda). 10 vols. The Hague, Martinus Nijhoff, 1950–62.

Locke, J., *Essay Concerning Human Understanding,* new ed., vols. 1–2. London, Dent, Everyman's Library, 1961.

Merleau-Ponty, Maurice, *La Phénoménologie de la perception.* Paris, N.R.F.–Gallimard, 1945.

Quine, W. V. O., *From a Logical Point of View.* New York, Harper Torchbooks, 1963.

Salmon, C. V., *The Central Problem of David Hume's Philosophy*. Halle, Max Niemeyer Verlag, 1929.

Sartre, Jean-Paul, *L'Être et le néant*. Paris, N.R.F.–Gallimard, 1943. (English translation by H. E. Barnes: *Being and Nothingness*. London, Methuen, 1957.)

Sartre, Jean-Paul, *L'Imaginaire*. Paris, N.R.F.–Gallimard, 1948.

Wiener, N., *Cybernetics*. Cambridge, Mass. M.I.T. 2nd ed., 1965.

SUBJECT INDEX

INDEX OF PHILOSOPHERS'
NAMES